Praise for T

MW00856903

"In recent years there has be........
authentic Catholic education. By chronicling the many success sto.... ..
schools who are leading the way, *The Catholic School Playbook* provides a
clear and practical blueprint for the future of Catholic education. This is
an extremely important book and a must-read for all Catholic educators. I
am convinced that unless Catholic schools move in the direction mapped
out in this book, they are doomed to fail."

—**Bishop James D. Conley**, Diocese of Lincoln

"*The Catholic School Playbook* is required reading for Catholics who know
that we are living in a time to build. Failing Catholic schools need to be re-
formed, and new Catholic schools need to be established. Michael Ortner
and Kimberly Begg provide readers with the data, stories, and first-person
accounts on building and sustaining an authentic Catholic school in the
midst of our current malaise. The result is a book that is as inspirational
as it is essential."

—**Ryan T. Anderson**, President of the Ethics and Public Policy Center

"Are you interested in being part of the renewal in Catholic education? *The
Catholic School Playbook* tells you how to score. A clear and concise and
encouraging book."

—**Dale Ahlquist**, President of the Society of Gilbert Keith Chesterton and
    editor of *The Everlasting Man: A Guide to G.K. Chesterton's Masterpiece*

"Catholic schools that are truly *Catholic* make a significant contribu-
tion to the New Evangelization and to the renewal of American culture.
Inner-city Catholic schools are the best anti-poverty program the Church
has ever devised. So the flourishing of Catholic schools is essential to both
the Church and the country. May the examples in this 'playbook' inspire
many others to take up this great cause."

—**George Weigel**, Distinguished Senior Fellow of the Ethics and
    Public Policy Center

"This volume is exactly what Catholic dioceses need at the present time,
when, after decades of decline, Catholic schools are undergoing fresh
demand and wondering how best to meet it. Michael Ortner and Kimberly Begg have produced a guidebook for school leaders that ranges
from the highest ideas and Christ-centered curricula to the nuts and

bolts of funding, community events, and parent involvement. Teachers and administrators who are overwhelmed by the secular demands of achievement and worldly success will find in *The Catholic School Playbook* tools that will help them resist those dehumanizing twenty-first-century trends. Most important of all, Ortner and Begg show the way to another kind of success, a school Catholic through and through, which is what so many parents have wanted all along. Every bishop in America who has seen his enrollments dropping and teachers leaving should take this book as an itinerary of recovery and flourishing."

—**Mark Bauerlein**, senior editor at *First Things* and Emeritus Professor of English at Emory University

"In these pages, Michael Ortner and Kimberly Begg weave the threads of the story of the renewal of Catholic education—a grassroots response to the prompting of the Holy Spirit—into a beautiful and compelling tapestry. Through the voices and experiences of parents, teachers, leaders, and thinkers, this comprehensive account not only delivers a coherent and convincing vision of Catholic education, but also provides a roadmap of practical steps for bishops, pastors, and school leaders who seek to align their schools more closely with the Church's distinct vision of education."

—**Mary Pat Donoghue**, Executive Director, Secretariat of Catholic Education, United States Conference of Catholic Bishops

"*The Catholic School Playbook* is the perfect guide to cut through the deafening noise of ideologies and self-perpetuating educational experimentation in order to help us recalibrate our mission as Catholic schools. It is a must-read from bishops to parents, and a plea to pastors and principals. It will resonate heartily with teachers, and, to be honest, it could also be a real help to the wider spectrum—from pope to student! Bravo to Ortner and Begg for consolidating wisdom which is 'ever ancient, ever new.'"

—**Michael Van Hecke**, President of the Institute for Catholic Liberal Education

"*The Catholic School Playbook* is the 'common sense' manifesto for Catholic education. It is the critical link between what has been a quiet, under-the-radar educational renewal movement in mainstream Catholic education. In a decade, every Catholic school administration will have read it."

—**Jeremy Tate**, Chief Executive Officer, Classic Learning Test

THE
CATHOLIC
SCHOOL
PLAYBOOK

THE CATHOLIC SCHOOL PLAYBOOK

MICHAEL ORTNER
AND KIMBERLY BEGG

WORD on FIRE.

Published by Word on Fire, Elk Grove Village, IL 60007
© 2025 by Michael Ortner and Kimberly Begg
Printed in the United States of America
All rights reserved

Cover design by Nicolas Fredrickson, typesetting by Marlene Burrell,
and interior art direction by Rozann Lee

Scripture excerpts are from the New Revised Standard Version Bible:
Catholic Edition (copyright © 1989, 1993), used by permission of the
National Council of the Churches of Christ in the United States of
America. All rights reserved worldwide.

Uncited quotations are taken directly from email communication
and used with permission

ISBN: 978-1-68578-208-5

Library of Congress Control Number: 2024941546

Contents

Boom to Bust to . . . Renewal?

AMERICA'S FIRST CATHOLIC SCHOOLS date back to at least 1606, when Franciscan friars opened a school in what is now St. Augustine, Florida. In 1782, St. Mary's in Philadelphia became the first parochial school in the United States, creating a tradition of Catholic education that proliferated in the 1800s and eventually peaked during the 1965–1966 school year, when approximately 5.7 million K–12 students (over 10% of all school-age children in the US) attended more than 12,000 Catholic schools.

Parents across all income levels and from a wide range of backgrounds chose Catholic schools for their children. The academic, moral, and spiritual formation provided by Catholic schools was perceived as at least equal to, and in some ways better than, what they could expect to receive at the free neighborhood public schools. By the numbers and despite long odds, Catholic education in the United States became a huge success story!

Unfortunately, times have changed since that high-water mark in 1965. Over the last sixty years, despite the number of self-identifying Catholics in the US growing by over 50%, Catholic school enrollment has plummeted by 75%, and over half of Catholic schools have closed. In the 2020–2021 school year, just 1.6 million students attended fewer than 6,000 Catholic schools. The last couple years have witnessed a slight uptick to 1.7 million students, but it remains to be seen whether this is a lasting positive trend or a minor reprieve related to public school closings during the pandemic.

So what happened? Is the collapse merely a symptom of the decline that the Catholic Church and Christianity more broadly have experienced within the US and much of the world? After all, the waning of the number of American religious sisters from 180,000 in 1965 to less than 50,000 today has had an enormous impact on the Catholic teaching profession. The loss of cheap labor has led directly to substantial tuition increases. And the steep declines in Catholic marriages, baptisms, and Mass attendance would seem to indicate that parents place less value on spiritual formation. No doubt, the struggles of the Catholic Church are a substantial reason for the decline of Catholic schools.

However, when you look closely at most Catholic schools that have survived, they not only appear very similar to the nearby public schools; they also seem different from what Catholic schools once were. Some changes, such as smaller class sizes, have been positive. Other changes have resulted in a less Catholic and less differentiated school experience. Sacraments are less frequent. Latin is no longer required, and often not taught at all. Classic texts—from Augustine to Aquinas to Dante—are no longer required reading and have largely disappeared. The schools have become less Catholic, both spiritually and intellectually. It's as if school leaders have forgotten what made attending Mass, learning Latin, and reading the classics so important. The focus has shifted from cultivation of virtue to college and career readiness with a growing presence of computers in the classroom, test-driven Advanced Placement classes, and a broad dumbing down of the curriculum.

But the news is not all bleak! In fact, we now have great cause for hope, not dissimilar from the prodigal son who lost and then found his way. Hundreds of Catholic schools across the country are not merely surviving in the twenty-first century; in fact, they are thriving. Parents who discover them are often thrilled at the formation and education their children are receiving, often to the point of benign envy once they realize how deficient their own education and faith formation were. These schools—some of which are startups and others turnarounds—have increasing enrollment, and, in many cases, waitlists of students eager to attend. More significantly, though, they have clearly differentiated themselves from both the local public and private schools. They have typically embraced the study of classic texts, Latin, grammar, art, poetry, and music, in addition to the typical staples of history, math, and science. They prioritize the cultivation of wonder and virtue over the trendy concerns of college and career readiness. They have remained—or in many cases returned to being—authentically Catholic. Perhaps most importantly, they hire teachers whose faith and own sense of wonder are evident, and who are able to transmit this passion to their students.

The Catholic School Playbook tells the stories of these successful Catholic schools and identifies their common themes so that other Catholic schools can follow their lead and contribute to a renewal of Catholic education in America.

CHAPTER I

Mission

THE HEART AND SOUL OF A SCHOOL

MISSION IS THE HEART AND SOUL of a school. It inspires its culture and curriculum, forms its students and teachers, and bonds its school families to one another.

Most modern educators understand mission in utilitarian terms: the aim of learning is not the pursuit of truth and human flourishing, but socialization and preparation for college and the workforce.

There is nothing wrong with wanting to prepare students for college and a career, but as the primary goal? That's too low of a bar and it cheats our children. In fact, all schools highlighted in this playbook share these objectives—but they do so as secondary goals, achieved through the authentically Catholic education of children made in the image and likeness of God. Ironically, by focusing on the education and formation of the whole person and basic skills such as reading, listening, writing, speaking, and thinking well, rather than on college and career readiness, the schools highlighted in this playbook *perform better* on the very metrics held up as paramount by many modern schools. This may seem counterintuitive. But it is only because it is countercultural.

For decades, school curricula and methods have evolved to reflect an increasingly secular worldview— one that sees the world through the distorted lens of materialism, progressivism, and the rejection of God and tradition.

As a result, classroom dynamics have changed dramatically over the years. Instead of encouraging students to grapple with the great ideas, events, and works of Western civilization, modern teachers build lessons around upcoming quantitative assessments. To some extent, this is an exercise in prudence. Teachers know they are evaluated not on students' understanding of the world and their place in it, or on their growth in faith and virtue, but on the compiled standardized test results for the class.

The utilitarianism of modern education is incompatible with the salvific goal of the Catholic Church. And yet, many Catholic schools today are indistinguishable from their secular counterparts; they've abandoned the rich intellectual tradition and sacramental life of the Church, replacing morality with relativism, wonder with pragmatism, and exploration with test preparation.

Michael Hanby is the Associate Professor of Religion and Philosophy of Science at the Pontifical John Paul II Institute for Marriage and Family Studies at the

Catholic University of America. He is also the principal author of the St. Jerome Educational Plan. He speaks of the need for

> a profound renewal of Catholic education and the recovery of a Catholic imagination. You cannot ultimately have a Catholic heart without a Catholic mind, and our children cannot be expected to *live* as Catholics if they cannot *think* and *see* as Catholics. We do not have a unified vision of Catholic education because we no longer have a Catholic vision of reality—of nature, the human being, and the meaning of history—and every vision of education puts into operation some basic conception of reality. The question is, "Which one?" To address the crisis in Catholic education, we must begin to come to terms with our own anonymous atheism.

He elaborates,

> We have never adequately thought through the question of what it really means to educate if Catholicism is true. This is a question of form and content, method and substance, and it rests on irreducibly philosophical answers to more fundamental questions about the nature of things and the meaning of history. . . . The loss of any intelligible sense of nature as something other than brute material or a machine is at the heart of our contemporary real crisis. After all, a world that really is known and loved into being

by God is in essence a very different place from the world conceived, in Chesterton's words, "as a dim and monstrous oval germ that laid itself by accident."

The mission problem of Catholic education is serious but solvable, as shown by school leaders across the country who have resisted outside pressures and even reversed damage inflicted on their school communities.

LEADERSHIP

It is impossible to overstate the importance of strong leadership in Catholic education. The best schools have passionate, virtuous leaders—principals and headmasters, pastors, board members, and superintendents—who shape the mission, culture, operations, and community makeup of schools and enable them to thrive.

Great leaders are, first and foremost, servant leaders modeled after Jesus Christ's sacrificial love in service of God's children. Jesus said to his disciples, "I am among you as one who serves" (Luke 22:27). He washed the feet of his disciples and told them they ought to wash each other's feet, explaining, "If I, your Lord and Teacher, have washed your feet, you also ought to wash one another's feet. For I have set you an example, that you also should do as I have done to you" (John 13:14–15). Servant leaders of a Catholic school must not serve selfish interests—for example, a prideful desire for power or praise. Rather, they must obey God and his Church in service of the school community and in accordance with the theological virtues of faith, hope, and charity and the cardinal virtues of prudence, justice, temperance, and fortitude.

Unlike Jesus Christ, the school leaders highlighted in this playbook are not perfect. They make mistakes, as all humans do. But they strive to be faithful, virtuous servants of God, are eager to learn how to better serve their school communities, and are unafraid to make changes—even when doing so invites the anger and ridicule of others—to advance a bold mission in cooperation with the universal Church.

CATHOLIC IDENTITY

Heidi Altman is principal of St. Mary's Catholic School, a Pre-K–11 (soon-to-be Pre-K–12) parochial school in Taylor, Texas, that was founded in 1876 by Dominican Sisters and that launched a high school with the help of the Chesterton Schools Network in 2020. When she became principal in the summer of 2016, she was handed an enrollment roster of fifty students and a decree by the bishop that the school would be closing after that year if enrollment didn't improve. Altman got to work reclaiming St. Mary's strong Catholic identity. After seven straight years of declining enrollment before she became principal, St. Mary's surpassed its twenty-year enrollment high by her fourth year (2019–2020). Enrollment is now 268 students with a waitlist, and new classroom space has been found in an old convent on campus that Altman renovated in 2021. "God brings forth miracles when you trust him and center all your efforts on his will!" she exclaims. She has advice for Catholic schools that have been influenced by modern education trends: "Sadly, I have noticed that many struggling schools are trying hard to keep up with the local public schools by following their programs and curriculum and then just adding Mass and a crucifix on the walls. . . . St. Mary's is different because we are not afraid to be who God calls us to be—an authentically, unabashedly *Catholic* school immersed in the (classical) intellectual tradition of the Church!"[1]

Andrew Shivone is the President of St. Jerome Institute (SJI), an independent high school in Washington, DC, that has "reinvented traditional education to meet the challenges of our time." Since its founding in 2019, SJI has developed a national reputation as a school for teachers who love to teach—and who understand that the cultivation of virtue in students is an important aspect of the profession. Shivone argues that

> one of the most tragic chapters in the history of Catholic education in the United States is the grow-ing divide in schools between faith and reason. Even when schools teach orthodox doctrine, it is often the case that the rest of the curriculum is built on philo-sophical presuppositions that rule out the possibility of faith. At most, the modern scientific mindset

1. "Educator Interview: Heidi Altman," Catholic School Playbook website, https://www.catholicschoolplaybook.com/interview-heidi-altman.

allows for faith only as a sort of emotional therapy. What it can never do is speak about what is most real, what is most interior to reality itself. When I taught theology, I remember students and parents getting upset if their students got anything less than an A in class. I remember being asked "How can you fail theology? It's not a real class." Underlying this was a basic belief that ran throughout the school that the Catholic faith was a matter of feeling, a matter of private opinion, and had nothing to do with reason or reality. Catholic schools must not only rethink their "religion" curriculum but the whole school in order that the faith might be lived in thought, word, and deed.

Elisabeth Sullivan is executive director of the Institute for Catholic Liberal Education (ICLE), a nonprofit organization dedicated to preserving and renewing K–12 Catholic schools. ICLE helps teachers, school leaders, and superintendents reclaim the Church's long tradition in the liberal arts and sciences, transforming parochial, diocesan, and independent schools around the country. Sullivan explains that an authentic, "unabashed" Catholic identity is what makes schools like St. Mary's thrive:

Thriving Catholic schools understand that their mission is, first and foremost, an extension of the mission of the universal Church: *to lead all to know, to love, and to live joyfully in the truth of Jesus Christ in this world and the next.* In support of parents as the

primary educators, these schools hope to help form
disciples whose faith, wisdom, and virtue will frame
lives of happiness and holiness, who will be a leaven
in the Church and the wider culture.[2]

What Sullivan describes is an approach to education
that is novel to most educators and families today. It
represents a true embrace of the Catholic Church.
Respect for parents as the primary educators of their
children is essential to this vision.

Julian Malcolm is headmaster of the Summit Academy, an independent high school in Fredericksburg,
Virginia, that also offers a hybrid (three days a week)
program for middle school students. Malcolm understands the mission of his school as "support[ing] parents
in their vocation as parents." He explains, "We operate
the school, but we're not the ones with the vocation to
raise their children. That's the parents' job and we are
here to support them."[3]

It turns out that support for parents as primary
educators is what many conscientious Catholic parents
are seeking in their children's education. And they're
willing to pay extra for it.

2. "Educator Interview: Elisabeth Sullivan," Catholic School
Playbook website, https://www.catholicschoolplaybook.com/interview
-elisabeth-sullivan.

3. "Educator Interview: Julian Malcolm," Catholic School Playbook website, https://www.catholicschoolplaybook.com/interview
-julian-malcolm.

Abby Sandel has been a parent at St. Jerome Academy, a parochial school in Hyattsville, Maryland, since 2009. She was present at St. Jerome Catholic Church when her pastor announced after Mass that their school would be closing if enrollment did not improve. She attended a meeting about the effort to save the school and was inspired by then-principal Mary Pat Donoghue's "reimagining" of the mission to embrace the longstanding educational tradition of the church. She now enthusiastically recommends St. Jerome Academy to other families. When asked why it is worth paying tuition at her Catholic school when public schools are free, Sandel explains,

> *Faith is not an extracurricular activity....* I can't imagine putting our children's faith formation on our family calendar as if it's just another soccer practice. Growing in faith, especially for children, means spending days in an environment where faith is practiced and modeled consistently.
>
> *It's simply not possible to have a full education without a faith perspective embedded in everything that is taught.* That's especially true with history and literature, but SJA faculty in science and art and every discipline have shaped our children's love of God and sense that they have a responsibility to something greater than themselves.[4]

4. "Parent Interview: Abby Sandel," Catholic School Playbook website, https://www.catholicschoolplaybook.com/interview-abby-sandel.

A major point of departure for faithful Catholic schools is their understanding of vocation as not just a career path but, in the words of St. John Henry Newman, a belief that God "has committed some work to me which He has not committed to another."

Catholic education should, as Malcolm offers, "be a hub for forming Catholic evangelists who have a real sense of vocation." He explains, "We aim to form free, joyful young men and women whose recognition of Christ as the Logos—the divine reason that calls creation into being, giving the world order, form, and meaning, and orienting it from and towards love—informs their understanding of what they're called to do in the world."[5]

BUILDING AN APOSTOLATE

Fr. Robert Sirico, founder of both the Acton Institute and the St. John Henry Newman Institute, became pastor of Sacred Heart of Jesus Parish in Grand Rapids, Michigan, a parish with a K–8 school, in 2012. The school had been in existence for 107 years—it opened in 1905 through the efforts of Polish immigrants seeking a Catholic education for their children—but it was struggling. Enrollment had plummeted to sixty-eight students and leadership had dwindled to the smallest it had ever been. The bishop gave Fr. Sirico permission to close the school if he wanted to. Fr. Sirico declined the offer and

5. "Julian Malcolm."

instead decided to observe the school and make changes consistent with his vision for the parish. Today, Sacred Heart Academy is a thriving K–12 parochial school that serves 380 students.

Fr. Sirico is quick to give credit to the headmaster, staff, and teachers for turning the school around. But he acknowledges the important role he played early on in articulating a clear vision that inspired key people to offer their help. The most important part of that vision was recasting the school as an apostolate of the parish—not, as some parishioners and members of the school community believed it to be, a mostly separate entity that relied on the parish for some financial assistance. He explains, "A school is an apostolate—the largest of a parish. If you view it that way, a school does not compete with a parish, it assists the parish. The formation of souls is the Church's mission and how it's done is a tactical decision."[6]

Once he made his vision known, Fr. Sirico began making changes at the school to better provide for the formation of souls. He replaced the leadership, hung beautiful art on the walls, and introduced a curriculum inspired by the great ideas and works of Western civilization. But the most important change he made—what became the single most important transformer of the school culture—was introducing daily Mass into the school day. Fr. Sirico moved the 8:00 a.m. Mass to 7:45

6. "Educator Interview: Fr. Robert Sirico," Catholic School Playbook website, https://www.catholicschoolplaybook.com/interview-fr-robert-sirico.

a.m. so students and teachers could worship alongside parishioners at the same quiet, contemplative service.

DAILY MASS

Rosemary Vander Weele is principal of Our Lady of Lourdes Catholic Classical School, a once-struggling Pre-K–8 parochial school in Denver, Colorado. Vander Weele increased enrollment from 90 to 351 students with a waitlist, adding a new campus to keep up with increased demand from families eager to be a part of a faithful Catholic community. She explains,

> My vision when I first became principal in 2011 was to reclaim the Catholic identity of the school. I had been teaching in Catholic schools for seven years and I was wrestling with why my students came back after they graduated embracing the same worldview as their public school counterparts. I was in graduate school at the Augustine Institute, writing my thesis on why Catholic education is failing. I became good friends with Bishop James Conley and was inspired by his conversion story. He became Catholic when he was introduced to truth, goodness, and beauty through Kansas University's Integrated Humanities Program in the 1970s. This is when I discovered how Catholicism is beautifully wed to classical education. But when I first started down this road, my biggest push was to do what we needed to do to get kids to live their faith post-graduation and want to continue

to be Catholic. That's what set our school on this path, and it remains the most important aspect of what I want to accomplish to this day.

Students at Our Lady of Lourdes attend Mass four days a week. Vander Weele shares, "When I first came to Lourdes, it was once a week. Five years in, we made the announcement that students would attend daily Mass and thirty-eight students left. That was tough because we were just getting our footing with enrollment. But by January of that school year, fifty new students enrolled because families said, 'Finally, here's a school that takes Mass seriously and makes it a priority!'"

Vander Weele says the whole culture of her school changed when she made the change to daily Mass. She explains,

> The sacramental grace of receiving communion every day is real; students are less inclined to not be virtuous. Now, we still have knucklehead kids, but, overall, our students are obedient and joyful. Kids like to pray. Our students actually say that Mass is their favorite part of the day. So, it's the direct opposite of what the families who left said would happen—that their kids would feel like they were going to Mass way too much. It's the exact opposite. They love going to Mass every day. In fact, the kids who graduate and come back after going to public high school say that's what they miss the most.

Starting the day with Mass becomes a habit. It becomes hard to miss it because you need it. The fruits have been incredible. It has confirmed our identity with families. They know our school is Catholic. This isn't a school that just teaches religion class for thirty-five minutes a day. This is the air we breathe. It's part of who we are. And it's why we are attracting students from much farther away than other schools. We have families from fifty zip codes at our school and they probably pass three other Catholic schools on their way here.[7]

Daily Mass is a draw for Catholic families across the country who are focused on their children's sanctity.

Daniel Ethridge is headmaster of Ville de Marie Academy, an independent K–12 school in Scottsdale, Arizona, that has full enrollment and a waitlist for every class. The main vision for his school "is for all students to develop a relationship with Christ that will last a lifetime—formed in Catholic tradition and informed in the teachings of the Church."[8] Daily Mass is an essential part of how Ville de Marie fulfills that vision—and it is what Ethridge says parents value most about his school.

7. "Educator Interview: Rosemary Vander Weele," Catholic School Playbook website, https://www.catholicschoolplaybook.com/interview -rosemary-vander-weele.

8. "Educator Interview: Daniel Ethridge," Catholic School Playbook website, https://www.catholicschoolplaybook.com/interview -daniel-ethridge.

PARTICIPATION IN THE LITURGICAL LIFE
OF THE CHURCH

The Catholic Church has a rich tradition of celebrating seasons, feasts, and saints throughout the year—to enhance the worship of Christ and bring deeper meaning and purpose to everyday experiences. Living liturgically in harmony with the universal Church has become a hallmark of many faithful Catholic schools. Here are some of the most beloved liturgical celebrations embraced by school communities throughout the school year:

Year-Round
Adoration
Confession

September
Nativity of the Blessed Virgin Mary

October
St. Thérèse of the Child Jesus
Holy Guardian Angels
Our Lady of the Rosary

November
All Saints Day
All Souls Day

December
Advent
Immaculate Conception of the Blessed
    Virgin Mary

Christmas (no school—family time)

January
Day of Prayer for the Legal Protection of
    Unborn Children

February to March
Ash Wednesday

March
St. Joseph Day
The Annunciation of the Lord

Lent
Stations of the Cross
Palm Sunday

Easter Triduum (no school—family time)
Easter

May
Pentecost
Visitation of the Blessed Virgin Mary
May Crowning

June
Corpus Christi

CATHOLIC FORMATION IN A SECULAR WORLD

As outlined in the USCCB's *Program of Priestly Formation*, priestly formation can be broken down into four dimensions: human (our relationships driven by Christian values), spiritual (our life of prayer, Scripture, and sacraments), intellectual (our understanding of the truth of the Christian faith), and pastoral (the ability to lead others to Christ). Catholic schools are well positioned to serve parents in a similar formation of their children so that they may eventually become spiritual leaders in their communities.

The Catholic worldview—rooted in the understanding that all humans are made in the image and likeness of God for the purpose of knowing, loving, and serving him, and spending eternity with him in heaven—is diametrically opposed to the version of reality endorsed by secular society. An authentic Catholic education, therefore, must not only pass on the truth of the faith; it must also keep the distortions of secularism out.

Mo Woltering is headmaster of Holy Family Academy, a K–12 independent school in Manassas, Virginia, with full enrollment and a waitlist, that offers daily Mass as the "centerpiece" of its curriculum and formation. Founded in 1993, Holy Family Academy has established a reputation for being faithfully and thoroughly

Catholic—which, in today's world, is as much about keeping out the harmful aspects of the culture as it is about passing on truth and tradition. He explains,

> While no other time in history exactly compares to our time now, there is no question that we are living through societal upheaval. In some ways it is similar to the time after the fall of the Western Roman Empire. During that time, monasteries all across Europe helped to preserve the treasures of our faith, intellectual heritage, and sacred liturgy. Our vision is to help Catholic families become like the monasteries of the so-called Dark Ages where the cultural treasures of our Catholic beliefs were preserved and passed on to future generations. . . . Monasteries have walls that are meant to keep certain things out. At the same time, St. Benedict instructed that the monks had an obligation to welcome anyone sincerely seeking peace and the Good.[9]

Even the "best" public schools and the majority of private schools cannot offer an education comparable to what Holy Family Academy and other faithful Catholic schools offer. That's because they do not teach the truth of Christianity. Rather, they teach a non-Christian worldview that distorts the teaching of all academic

---

9. "Educator Interview: Mo Woltering," Catholic Schools Playbook website, https://www.catholicschoolplaybook.com/interview-mo-woltering.

subjects, thus obscuring fundamental truths about the nature of man and all aspects of the human experience.

C.S. Lewis said, "Christianity . . . if false, is of *no* importance, and if true, of infinite importance. The one thing it cannot be is moderately important."[10]

All public schools (including charter schools) and many private schools are prohibited from teaching the truth of Christianity: that Jesus Christ is the fully human, fully divine Son of God whose life, death, and Resurrection fulfilled the prophecies of the Old Testament and opened the gates of heaven to those who love God and follow his commandments. These schools are not neutral on Christianity. Rather, they teach values that are hostile to the faith—for example, that Christianity is anti-science and bigoted, that abortion is health care, that gender is independent of biological sex, and that promiscuity among all people, including children and young adults, should be encouraged.

Not all families seeking Catholic education are Catholic, but they all have an important distinction in common: they have opted their children out of the "free" public schools in favor of *paying for* religious education. Catholic schools that teach that Christianity is "of infinite importance" in confronting progressive cultural trends earn the confidence of these families; by passing on the timeless truths and traditions of the Catholic

10. C.S. Lewis, "Christian Apologetics," in *God in the Dock: Essays on Theology and Ethics*, ed. Walter Hooper (Grand Rapids, MI: Eerdmans, 1970), 102.

Church, they develop strong communities of families who grow together in faith and love for one another.

TECHNOLOGY

Catholic schools that are serious about forming disciples must be intentional about rejecting the most harmful aspects of the culture. No threat poses more danger to children today than the prevalence of smartphones and other technology in the daily lives of Americans.

Deacon Christopher Roberts is president of Martin Saints Classical High School, an independent high school in Oreland, Pennsylvania, that is a part of the Chesterton Schools Network. Martin Saints seeks to "pass the Catholic faith to our students by rendering a portrait of the faith that is as plausible, compelling, and beautiful as possible." Deacon Roberts does this by playing "offense and defense." He says he spends most of his time on "offense," which he describes as "cultivating our students' imagination by running towards all that is good, true, and beautiful." Protecting students from technology represents a major part of his "defense." He explains,

> Defense means rejecting the unwholesome influences of the culture. We caution our school families against being on autopilot with technology and media consumption. Nothing good comes from unsupervised internet access, especially alone in bedrooms at night. But perhaps less obviously, the

risk with technology isn't just wasting time, online bullying, or pornography. There's also the issue of how it warps our capacity for attention and gets us addicted to constant stimulation. If we're trying to cultivate students who can think as well as pray, we need students who have at least some familiarity with interior stillness and silence.[11]

Best practices relating to technology use include:

- Ban personal devices at school. Many schools forbid K–8 students from bringing devices to school at all and allow high school students to keep phones in their bags or lockers during the school day (but do not allow high school students to use personal laptops, tablets, or phones in class). The accommodation for phones is made for older students to coordinate rides and for other responsible purposes.
- Keep computers out of the classroom (or wait until high school to introduce limited computer instruction). Many schools have technology-free classrooms through eighth grade and offer limited exposure in high school consistent with liberal education—for example, offering computer science, but only for older students after they have been exposed to Latin and logic, which cultivates

11. "Educator Interview: Deacon Christopher Roberts," Catholic Schools Playbook website, https://www.catholicschoolplaybook.com /interview-christopher-roberts.

ordered thinking in young people better than pre-
mature computer training.

- Educate parents about the dangers posed by tech-
nological devices. Leaders should be in constant
communication with parents about this important topic.

Woltering recently advised his school parents to read
a book on this topic—*Digital Minimalism: Choosing a
Focused Life in a Noisy World* by Cal Newport. He offered
three warnings to parents: (1) Devices are designed to be
addictive. For young people especially, their relationship
with devices and social media becomes like going back
to the slot machine to see if one more pull will win the
jackpot. Young people need parents to set boundaries to
identify and prevent future harm caused by this addiction. (2) Texting is not conversation. Young people who
communicate exclusively through technology become
uncomfortable with in-person social situations; they
lack the refined skills to communicate effectively in
person. (3) Interacting with a screen is a passive activity.
It saps energy, while real leisure is invigorating. Young
people who spend time on devices are being robbed of
the opportunity to develop habits of pursuing healthy,
leisurely activities.

A "secret" of successful Catholic schools is that
they reject modern cultural trends that are boring and
harmful, opting instead to engage young people on an
educational journey that is good, true, and beautiful—as
well as contemplative and invigorating!

CULTIVATING VIRTUE

Dr. Mark Newcomb is the headmaster of Holy Rosary Academy, a Pre-K–12 independent school in Anchorage, Alaska, that "assists parents, the primary educators, to form students in faith, reason, and virtue through a classical education in the Roman Catholic Tradition." He previously served as principal of St. Theresa Catholic School, a Pre-K–8 classical parochial school in Sugar Land, Texas, for six years. Under his leadership, St. Theresa received the highest honor from the Ruah Woods Institute as a Theology of the Body campus, won a 2020 National Blue Ribbon award, and celebrated record enrollment.

Newcomb is a servant leader who aspires to pass on a spirit of servant leadership to his students. He explains, "We become free and full human persons only when we recognize the needs of others and serve them in the spiritual and corporal works of mercy, as informed by our authentic encounters with the risen Christ in Scripture and the sacraments."

He has a deep respect for parents as the primary educators of their children. He understands his vocation as an educator as assisting parents in their vocation as parents—and he knows that parenting has become increasingly complicated in recent years. He cites the use of screens as "a digital security blanket" and a chief cause of "the American breakdown in expectations and norms for young people today." He says the internet and social media "lower impulse control in children, addict them to peer validation as their primary way of determining what to do or not do, and serves to make them facile, in that all things and actions either get a thumbs up or a thumbs down."

He notes that sometimes it is the parents themselves who need to be educated about how to live a Christian life. Throughout his time in Catholic education, he has observed that "even believing Christian families often do not connect care for others with their faith, but rather hold to a vague sense of civic responsibility or character, without reference to the love and salvific mission of Jesus Christ."

When Newcomb arrived in Anchorage in 2021, one of his goals was to get ahead of problems that have plagued other schools by assisting parents in forming kind, charitable, and virtuous children. He notes that his school already had a culture rooted in truth, goodness, and beauty that predated him, and his efforts have only deepened his school community's commitment to supporting each other in the cultivation of virtue.

To encourage students, teachers, and parents to personalize the teachings of Jesus Christ, Newcomb introduced the "Knight's Code," a character charter of twelve virtues "drawn from the treasury of the wisdom of Christendom." Named for the school's mascot— because knights are "supposed to come to the rescue of those who are being mistreated"—the code not only sets expectations for behavior at school but also shapes the way students understand their duty to God and each other. The virtues, as enumerated for student expectations at Holy Rosary Academy, are:

1. **Fidelity**—exhibits a love of God and his Church
2. **Charity**—is kind and helpful with others; courteous in speech, word, and deed
3. **Justice**—willingly meets duties and follows all school rules; seeks the common good
4. **Sagacity**—uses time, resources, and talents wisely
5. **Prudence**—exercises good judgment in managing and organizing own affairs
6. **Temperance**—maintains good impulse control; is punctual and responsible
7. **Resolution**—is determined and resilient in the face of challenges
8. **Truthfulness**—is rigorously honest and honorable in all academic and personal matters
9. **Liberality**—is self-sacrificing and generous in the service of others
10. **Diligence**—seeks to do the right thing at the right time; attentive and studious
11. **Hope**—has a positive outlook about self and encouraging attitude towards others
12. **Valor**—is courageous in promoting and protecting the interests of others

Newcomb integrated the Code into the school's discipline system, which had previously focused on demerits. Holy Rosary Academy still gives demerits for inappropriate behavior at school, especially when that behavior violates the dignity of another child. For example, teachers "intercede the moment that it appears that a student is not being treated with dignity and respect as made in the image and likeness of God, by his or her peers." But now, in addition to giving demerits, teachers award students "acts of valor" for conspicuously virtuous deeds. Every month, Holy Rosary Academy uses this system to recognize students for their goodness at an assembly attended by all teachers and students.

Newcomb reports that parents and teachers have been "*very*" enthusiastic about the Knight's Code because it connects home and school life and reinforces a culture that "celebrates the good, rather than merely castigating the bad."

He, too, is enthusiastic about the approach because he knows better formation of students requires better formation of teachers and parents. He explains, "Our goal is to form students who think first of others and who are here to serve one another. This requires each of us—faculty, staff, and parents included—to be willing to become better people, so that we can in time be a blessing to ourselves and those around us. None of this happens through stasis and low standards."[12]

Peter Crawford is the founding headmaster of St. Jerome Institute (SJI), which designed its curriculum and

12. Kimberly Begg, "Parents Expect Catholic Schools to Live Up to Their Rhetoric," Catholic School Playbook website, August 15, 2022, https://www.catholicschoolplaybook.com/post/parents-expect-catholic-schools-to-live-up-to-their-rhetoric.

culture with parents in mind. Informed by the Catholic principle that parents, not the government, are the primary educators of their children, SJI's founders created a school that personalizes the teachings of Jesus Christ to each child. They have a special appreciation for the freedom to help children make connections between their behavior and their responsibilities to God. Before becoming the headmaster of SJI, Crawford taught at three classical charter schools, two of which he founded. At those schools, he was prohibited by law from using Sacred Scripture, the *Catechism of the Catholic Church*, saints' writings, and other Christian sources to teach virtue.

At SJI, Crawford has used his freedom to give parents what they want and deserve: a partner in forming children who imitate Christ in their interactions with others. Under the light of truth, SJI prioritizes the cultivation of virtue in four essential ways. The school leader:

1. Hires, trains, and coaches teachers to model virtue and provide personalized mentorship to students.
2. Sets a single, unified expectation for student action and behavior that applies in all classrooms and all situations schoolwide.
3. Speaks to students and parents at the beginning of every school year about the school's philosophy regarding student action and behavior.

4. Finds opportunities to have conversations with students and parents, individually and in groups, to reinforce expectations throughout the year.

Crawford notes that all actions directed at a child must be motivated by love—the Christian duty to will the good of another. "It is not enough for parents and teachers to know that the reason we hold children accountable is because we love them," he says. "Children need to be explicitly told this." For love of the child, it is critical that parents and teachers demand good behavior to help establish habits of goodness. He explains, "Most people think that the way to derive a certain outcome from children is to win them over so they will start acting in the way that you want. Unfortunately, this is not how human behavior works. As Aristotle and modern psychology both agree, if you want to impact the interior life, you need to begin by making certain demands on human action. A requirement for consistent right action leads to right habits."[13]

Shivone adds, "Scripture makes quite clear the relationship between discipline and love. God himself disciplines. Hebrews says, 'The Lord disciplines the one he loves, and he chastens everyone he accepts as his son.' When we sever these two things, as often happens in schools, we find either a mindless rule-following or loveless permissiveness."

---

13. Kimberly Begg, "Parents Expect."

Crawford further explains that virtue is traditionally understood to mean habits of excellence. The key to obtaining virtuous behavior in children is having clear expectations and consistent accountability rooted in the truth, goodness, and beauty of Christ's sacrificial love.

THE TRANSCENDENTALS

A Catholic school's primary mission is to help form (some would even say liberate) its students in order that they direct their attention to seeking out what is true, good, and beautiful. These transcendental properties of being, as observed by Plato, Aristotle, Augustine, and Aquinas, among others, are all aspects of reality that lead us closer to God. We are called to know, desire, and love truth, goodness, and beauty. Schools accomplish this by cultivating virtues—habits of excellence—in students with the help of families and the Church. In fact, schools play a supportive role, not the primary role. Parents, as the first teachers of their children, are responsible for forming them in all of the virtues—spiritual, physical, moral, and intellectual. Schools can and should help with the formation of each of these types of virtues, but take primary responsibility for the intellectual virtues such as knowledge, understanding, and, eventually, wisdom.

Well-cultivated virtues are the path to seeking the transcendentals, to encountering God, and coming to know and love Jesus. That is the path to a flourishing life. That is the mission of Catholic schools.

CHAPTER 2

Pedagogy and Curriculum

THE HOW AND WHAT A SCHOOL TEACHES

WHEN ROOTED IN CHRISTIAN ANTHROPOLOGY and the Church's educational tradition, a school's pedagogy and curriculum transform learning into an adventure, empowering children to discover wondrous connections and order in the world and helping them understand their unique vocation as a child of God.

Michael Van Hecke is president of St. Augustine Academy, a K–12 independent school in Ventura, California, that "assists parents in their duty of fostering within their children growth in the theological, intellectual, and moral virtues." He is also president and founder of the Institute for Catholic Liberal Education and president and publisher of the Catholic Textbook Project, a company producing the first history textbooks specifically for Catholic schools in nearly fifty years.

St. Augustine Academy has full enrollment with a waitlist. Van Hecke explains what sets his school's curriculum and pedagogy apart from other schools: "Everything we do—intellectually, socially, culturally, etc.—derives from our creation as a child of God destined to spend eternity with Him in heaven. The faith is the substratum of all, and actually is the biggest motivational factor to study all disciplines well, for in them is truth. The more we understand truth the more we understand Truth."[1]

A deep appreciation for the truth that all human beings are made in the image and likeness of God—not merely cosmic accidents—is what inspires the most successful Catholic schools to embrace the classical tradition of liberal education as developed by the Church over the last two thousand years. This tradition includes the exploration of truth, goodness, and beauty—as originating from God and revealed through the study of the humanities, fine arts, sciences, and mathematics—in a manner that cultivates wonder.

CULTIVATING WONDER

St. Augustine said, "Here are men going afar to marvel at the heights of mountains, the mighty waves of the sea, the long courses of great rivers, the vastness of the ocean, the movements of the stars, yet leaving

---

1. "Educator Interview: Michael Van Hecke," Catholic School Playbook website, https://www.catholicschoolplaybook.com/interview-michael-van-hecke.

themselves unnoticed."[2] It is unnatural for children not to wonder about the mountains, the seas, and all of God's created world, not to mention about themselves and God's plan for their lives. Many teachers don't know that. They may have gone into teaching with a burning desire to inspire their students, but all they've ever known in the classroom is the pressure of the next set of assessments. They believe education is supposed to be boring because their students have always been bored.

But—as teachers across the country who are being trained to cultivate wonder in their classrooms are discovering—children love to learn when their natural sense of wonder is respected and nurtured.

Elisabeth Sullivan shares the enthusiasm of teachers who are rediscovering the art of their craft: "Teachers are attending not just to what they teach, but also how they teach—in a way that restores wonder and inquiry to the classroom. In doing so, they respect the dignity of the children, whose hunger to know is ultimately a hunger for God. By contrast, the industrialized model of cram, test, and forget produces apathy and anxiety. It does not feed the soul."

The result, Sullivan says, is a "palpable joy in learning." She explains, "Learning becomes an adventure to discover wondrous connections and order in the world God made, and to understand our unique vocation in this particular time and place. Children are engaged

2. St. Augustine, *Confessions*, trans. F.J. Sheed (Park Ridge, IL: Word on Fire Classics), 241.

by meaningful lessons, even in their youngest years. Students of all abilities and backgrounds thrive with a highly ordered introduction to reality; they learn how to learn in accord with their nature and development. It is natural, and it is fun."[3]

DISCUSSION METHOD

The discussion method is a style of teaching that facilitates logical thinking and dialogue through the practice of asking questions. Many Catholic schools, particularly high schools, utilize the discussion method—especially in seminar-style classes—to cultivate wonder and engage students as active participants in their own education. Students are seated in a rectangle facing each other as opposed to all facing the same direction.

Use of the discussion method is a signature element of a St. Jerome Institute education, which strives to situate students "within a community of learners, in a posture of wonder before the deep realities they are engaging." Peter Crawford's teachers take the craft of teaching—what he calls his faculty's "communal work of art"—seriously. They are eager to help students "actively wrestle with their studies" by asking good questions.

"But what constitutes a good question?" Crawford asks. He reflects,

3. "Educator Interview: Elisabeth Sullivan," Catholic School Playbook website, https://www.catholicschoolplaybook.com/interview -elisabeth-sullivan.

How can a question, or series of questions, directly lead students to engage with the reality they are studying? Are there ways of asking or types of questions that allow students of different levels and abilities to simultaneously engage subject matter? What are the risks of teaching through asking and how can these risks be mitigated? In other words, what are the distinct strategies and tactics of our craft? These are the sorts of considerations that the faculty of SJI take seriously. We ponder these matters as a group, lead each other in lessons, and are in a constant state of discussion about the craft of our art.[4]

INTEGRATION OF DISCIPLINES

One of the most important curricular differences of renewed Catholic schools is the integration of disciplines—in Christ and with each other—to provide a cohesive learning experience.

Crawford uses the imagery of a symphony, where "every class is in chordal harmony with every other," to illustrate how St. Jerome Institute's integrated curriculum helps students encounter "a meaningful whole": "The classes are integrated with one another so that each school day acts like a progression of chords. Together,

---

4. "Educator Interview: Peter Crawford," Catholic School Playbook website, https://www.catholicschoolplaybook.com/interview-peter-crawford.

the entire school day becomes one single lesson, as does the school year and the entire four-year curriculum."

Crawford shares an example of how students' classes are "regularly in dialogue" with each other: "Students start their ratio units in the Mathematics Seminar and promptly enter the music classroom to explore the circle of fifths. As students explore the navigational challenge of ascertaining longitude in Philosophy of Nature, they travel with Odysseus across the sea back to Ithaca in Humanities. As they contemplate the restless heart that longs for God in the beginning of the *Confessions*, they consider Caravaggio's masterpiece *The Conversion of St. Paul*."[5]

Students learn better—and with greater joy—when they understand how subjects relate to each other and how, together as a whole, they reveal the order and beauty of the human experience.

THE BUILDING BLOCKS OF AN INTEGRATED CURRICULUM

In 2009, under the leadership of then-principal Mary Pat Donoghue, St. Jerome Academy abandoned its disconnected curriculum, creating and implementing its own plan known as the Educational Plan of St. Jerome Academy. The school is not proprietary about its curriculum. On the contrary, it shares its plan freely and broadly, encouraging other schools to adopt

5. "Peter Crawford."

it wholly or use it for inspiration. For years, St. Jerome Academy's leadership and staff have made themselves available to answer questions and provide guidance to Catholic educators interested in transitioning or renewing their schools. Donoghue has been a particularly important resource for school leaders. After leaving St. Jerome Academy, she served as director of school services for the Institute for Catholic Liberal Education. She is now executive director of the Secretariat of Catholic Education for the United States Conference of Catholic Bishops.

Building on the experiences of school leaders and teachers with a passion for Catholic liberal education, and incorporating the ideas of great thinkers including Pope Benedict XVI, Archbishop J. Michael Miller, C.S. Lewis, Christopher Dawson, Peter Kreeft, Scott Hahn, and others, the Educational Plan of St. Jerome Academy provides for the integrated teaching of the following eight core subjects:

1. History
2. Religion
3. Art
4. Language Arts: Literature, Grammar, Composition, Logic, Latin, and Drama
5. Nature Studies: Science, Philosophy, and Theology
6. Mathematics
7. Music
8. Physical Education

The teaching of these core subjects to form a child's mind and character "in such a way that he can live his whole life, so far as possible, in a way that is consistent with the truth about himself as a human being created in the image and likeness of God" is a hallmark of renewed Catholic schools, whether they have adopted the Educational Plan of St. Jerome Academy or created their own curriculum inspired by the principles of Catholic liberal education.[6]

HISTORY

Andrew Zwerneman, president of Cana Academy and author of *History Forgotten and Remembered*, calls attention to a significant problem in our society that has been created by modern education's lack of context and cohesiveness in the teaching of history. He reveals, "As a society, we are increasingly divided from our past, which is a significant part of why we are increasingly divided from one another. To put it another way: There is a real sense in which history has been forgotten; and having forgotten our past, we have forgotten ourselves."[7]

Zwerneman recommends that Catholic schools confront this problem head-on by teaching students

6. St. Jerome Curriculum Group, "The Educational Plan of St. Jerome Academy," Catholic Liberal Education website, https://my.catholicliberaleducation.org/wp-content/uploads/2020/10/The-Educational-Plan-of-SJA-2020-edition.pdf.

7. Andrew Zwerneman, *History Forgotten and Remembered* (Falls Church, VA: Cana Academy, 2020), 8.

to see the past "in its pastness" and seek the truth of historical events as they occurred and not through a lens that either reduces the past to less than what it is or imposes meaning on history from beyond history. On this last point, Zwerneman says we can speak only of meaning in history since history is not yet complete. His approach to the study of history requires two essential habits. One, the study should be observational, where observation leads to understanding. The method is basically inductive. Students should especially work through the eruptive events that break into the ordinary flow of time and that have become the principal events we remember. Two, the study of history should be sympathetic: students should "suffer with" those who came before us, who shaped our world, and passed on our culture to us. Together, observation and sympathy form what Zwerneman calls a liberal approach to history, where "liberal" (from the Latin for "free") is understood in its classical meaning as the freedom to know the truth, to live by noble purpose, and to give generously of one's life to others as our forebears gave us the world we inhabit. The study of history cultivates classical freedom by focusing on the limited but glorious features of the human condition; the mysterious unity of the dead, the living, and those yet to come; and the power of human memory to collect what we know and love, as St. Augustine, the Church's greatest philosopher of history, so beautifully taught us.

An approach that is growing in popularity is teaching history chronologically and fully, without removing the consequential events of Christianity that have been filtered out of most modern education—most significantly, the Incarnation. Many K–8 Catholic schools cycle students twice through the history of ancient civilizations, the modern age, and America, beginning in kindergarten to fifth grade, and again in sixth to eighth grade, all the while calling students to:

1. see all of history and all cultures as expressions of the human desire for God, and
2. learn the stories of Western civilization and Christianity, which are intertwined and cannot be understood apart from each other.

Early on in the Catholic liberal education movement, educators had few resources to help them teach history free from secular distortions. Thanks to enterprising writers and publishers who have helped compile the good work of teachers and historians in recent years, that is no longer the case. Today, materials from trusted sources—including the Catholic Textbook Project's history books and TAN's *The Story of Western Civilization*—allow teachers to develop courses that are engaging, historically accurate, and oriented to truth.

A CHRIST-CENTERED CURRICULUM

A cornerstone of all thriving Catholic schools is the teaching of religion as "not just one subject within the curriculum, but the key to its unity and integration."[8]

A Christ-centered curriculum nurtures in children a deep love of the faith; it also helps them find order and meaning across all disciplines and experiences. Sullivan explains,

> Integration of knowledge, culture, faith, reason, and virtue are the essence of authentic Catholic education because we know that—though it is a mystery—all things are one in Christ. This is what feeds the soul. This is what helps us grow into integrated human beings. This is what helps us discover meaning in the things around us.
>
> Moreover, a key measure of the mind's power is the ability to make connections across disciplines and experience. An intellect that has been trained to detect pattern and order has an advantage in almost any career, including medicine, law, engineering, sports, carpentry, music, etc. And, these discoveries are delightful![9]

Today, many of the most successful Catholic schools are ones that only recently reoriented their schools

---

8. St. Jerome Curriculum Group, "Educational Plan."
9. "Elisabeth Sullivan."

with Christ at the center; they quickly discovered that unifying and integrating their curriculum around "the way, and the truth, and the life" (John 14:6) changed everything.

ART

G.K. Chesterton observed that humans, who are made in the image and likeness of God, are creators by nature because God is the Creator. By creating art that reflects the goodness, truth, and beauty of God's created world, man acts in accordance with his purpose of loving, serving, and worshiping him.

Secular society understands art, not as worship, but as "the conscious use of skill and creative imagination especially in the production of aesthetic objects."[10] Notice the breadth of this Merriam-Webster definition. "Aesthetic objects" need not be good, true, or beautiful to qualify as art. They need not even be interesting. They merely must be the result of "skill" and "creative imagination" that is "conscious." Thus, most "art" programs for children are exercises in aimless self-expression, with no regard for the transcendentals or the pursuit of human flourishing.

The study of art at renewed schools, on the other hand, cultivates "an appreciation of beauty, not merely as a subjective preference, as pretty or pleasant, but as an

---

10. *Merriam-Webster*, s.v. "art (*n.*)," accessed April 19, 2024, https://www.merriam-webster.com/dictionary/art.

objective feature of reality that expresses the deep truth of what things are."[11] Creating beautiful art is deeply formative for children. It is also deeply satisfying for them because it is consistent with their nature.

LANGUAGE ARTS

The Gospel of John begins with these words: "In the beginning was the Word, and the Word was with God, and the Word was God" (John 1:1). It proceeds to tell the story of Jesus: "And the Word became flesh and lived among us, and we have seen his glory, the glory as of a father's only son, full of grace and truth. (John testified to him and cried out, 'This was he of whom I said, "He who comes after me ranks ahead of me because he was before me."') From his fullness we have all received, grace upon grace. The law indeed was given through Moses; grace and truth came through Jesus Christ" (John 1:14–17).

Language arts is the study of words and the art of communication. Until recently, all societies in all times placed great emphasis on the passing down of words and stories aimed at educating, training, and socializing young people. This was true even when most men and women were not taught how to read and write. In recent decades, however, many schools have reduced the teaching of language arts to the instruction of basic reading and writing skills, with little to no regard for the mastery of language, parables, fairy tales, historical

11. St. Jerome Curriculum Group, "Educational Plan."

texts, and great works of literature and poetry that once formed a common bond among people of all ages.

There is a growing movement to reclaim the lost teaching of language arts by immersing young people in the study of Grammar, Composition, Literature, Drama, Logic, and Latin. Janice Martinez, principal of Holy Child Catholic School, a Pre-K–8 parochial school in Tijeras, New Mexico, explains, "I believe the classical education movement is going to save the Church and the nation, including non-Christians. . . . It's going to open up our imagination to what's good and beautiful. It's going to make us human again."

Martinez revels in the teaching of language arts—especially in the telling of stories through literature and poetry, which begins at her school when a child enters preschool. She explains, "For over two thousand years, we have been teaching our young the meaning of life through the tales of heroes like Achilles, Odysseus, and Aeneas. The Christian world carried on this tradition, adding the lives of saints and chivalric heroes like Beowulf and Arthur. These tales powerfully depict their quest for virtue with universal appeal."

Modern educators have vastly underestimated the benefit of introducing quality material to young children. In addition to enriching their minds with beautiful words and gripping themes, exposing young children to good works—including good books—prepares children's minds for more challenging texts and the "great books" as they grow.

Children have great capacity to grasp patterns in language. That's why it is considered a best practice to begin exposing children to Latin and other foreign languages at a young age—through instruction at school and home. Children who know English grammar—who can identify nouns, pronouns, adjectives, and other parts of speech—are well positioned to begin studying Latin as early as third grade; memorization of vocabulary and phrases can begin in kindergarten. Educators who wait to expose students to Latin until high school, instead of easing them into Latin grammar and vocabulary at a young age, put their students at a disadvantage; the same is true for other foreign languages, although, for spoken languages, the rule is to begin as early as possible, even in infancy. Studies show it is best for children to begin learning a foreign language by age ten to achieve the fluency of a native speaker.

Martinez has been delighted to see her students respond enthusiastically to the teaching of Latin beginning in kindergarten. She explains why Latin makes up an important part of her school's language arts curriculum:

> There are many benefits to the study of Latin. Besides the fact that half of English is derived from Latin, it is also important that it forms a precise and orderly mind in the young person. It is formational, not just informational. Its orderly structure develops the mind in such a way that it promotes logical thinking, problem solving skills, discipline, and general

order. Indeed, it is the missing component in modern education. Finally, it is the language of Western civilization and the Roman Catholic Church. If we really want to be rooted in our history, reading from the original language brings an intimacy with the culture that a translation does not transmit.

Modern educators often assume that because children are bored and perform poorly at modern schools, they would be more bored and perform even worse at schools that challenge them. Great Catholic schools show that nothing could be further from the truth—especially regarding a traditional language arts curriculum—as long as the education works in harmony with, and not against, a child's good and curious nature.

NATURE STUDIES: SCIENCE, PHILOSOPHY, AND THEOLOGY

An area of significant curricular departure for renewed Catholic schools is the teaching of nature studies—an integrated exploration of science, philosophy, and theology—that fosters in students an understanding of the created world and their place in it. Nature studies are the study of a "comprehensive vision of reality as God's creation."[12]

Children are fascinated by the natural world. They enjoy observing insects, birds, and other animals. They

12. St. Jerome Curriculum Group, "Educational Plan."

like gazing at the night sky. What they don't particularly enjoy—and what most modern schools require of them in science class—is memorizing terms and facts from a textbook, with no opportunity to observe the subject matter up close.

A common practice in renewed Catholic schools is granting children the freedom to explore the natural world—to walk in the woods, scoop up living creatures in a creek, and observe animals in their natural habitat. A favorite activity for many children is recording observations of plants and animals in a nature journal. Children enjoy drawing pictures and jotting down descriptions of what they see; they also enjoy looking back on what they had observed in previous weeks and seasons throughout the year. The more hands-on and personalized the studying of science can be—especially for young children, who have a natural curiosity about the natural world—the greater it will cultivate wonder and lead to mastery of the material.

Most modern teachers lack the freedom to tap into a child's natural curiosity because they are told their primary goal is to prepare students for quantitative assessments. Guided by considerations of efficiency, they use textbooks that cover the material students "need to know" and they test students on a multitude of terms and facts to "get them ready" for the final test. The textbooks contain no information connecting scientific facts with the vast body of knowledge outside of modern scientific methods; teachers neglect to make these connections on their own because they lack the education, will, or time to do so. As a result, students develop an incomplete understanding of the world and of science, which they fail to recognize as the joyful discovery of God's created world.

Catholic schools are finding that a combination of science, philosophy, and theology provides a better framework than science alone for the serious consideration of the study of nature. While some schools teach these subjects as distinct though integrated classes, others cover these topics together within a nature studies class, humane letters sequence, or great books seminar.

MATHEMATICS

No subject promotes logical thought in a child quite like mathematics. (Latin would be a close second!) Unfortunately, many children simply don't like math—at least they don't like the way most modern schools teach math. A 2018 Texas Instruments Education Technology survey found that 24% of American children "hate" or "dislike" math and another 30% are "indifferent" to math.[13] With a majority of young people lacking a positive attitude toward math, it's no surprise that the United States ranks thirty-seventh in the world in math literacy. A 2018 Stanford study confirms what math teachers at Catholic schools have observed for years: students with a positive attitude toward math perform better at math.

13. Peter Balyta, "Survey Says: Kids Like Math!" Texas Instruments website, August 28, 2018, https://education.ti.com/en/bulletinboard/2018/august/studentsurvey.

The study found that a positive attitude boosts the brain's memory center and predicts math performance independent of IQ.[14]

A strong foundation in arithmetic in elementary school is critical to a student's ability to eventually enjoy math since, likely more than any other subject, the concepts continue to build on each other. Students need to master each concept and then continue to be exposed to early concepts repeatedly as is promoted in textbooks like Saxon Math and Beast Academy.

Mathematician Paul Lockhart wrote a ground-breaking essay in 2002—"A Mathematician's Lament"—describing mathematics as the "purest of the arts, as well as the most misunderstood."[15] He criticized the standard teaching of math as "formulaic," "senseless," "soul-crushing," and "boring." He explains, "Students learn that mathematics is not something you do, but something that is done to you. Emphasis is placed on sitting still, filling out worksheets, and following directions. Children are expected to master a complex set of algorithms . . . unrelated to any real desire or curiosity on their part."

Lockhart said that bad teaching is due, in part, to the problem that educators don't know what mathematics

14. Erin Digitale, "Positive Attitude Toward Math Predicts Math Achievement in Kids," Stanford Medicine website, January 24, 2018, https://med.stanford.edu/news/all-news/2018/01/positive-attitude-toward-math-predicts-math-achievement-in-kids.html.

15. Paul Lockhart, *A Mathematician's Lament* (New York: Bellevue Literary Press, 2009), 22.

is. He explains, "Mathematics is the *art of explanation*. If you deny students the opportunity to engage in this activity—to pose their own problems, to make their own conjectures and discoveries, to be wrong, to be creatively frustrated, to have inspiration, and to cobble together their own explanations and proofs—you deny them mathematics itself. So no, I'm not complaining about the presence of facts and formulas in our mathematics classes; I'm complaining about the lack of *mathematics* in our mathematics classes."[16]

Catholic schools are at the forefront of an exciting movement bringing the art of mathematics back to the classroom to "instill in students an ever-increasing sense of wonder and awe at the profound way in which the world displays order, pattern and relation." They teach mathematics "not because it is first useful and then beautiful, but because it reveals the beautiful order inherent in the cosmos."[17]

St. Jerome Institute is a school on the cutting edge of the teaching of mathematics that offers students unique opportunities to appreciate the beauty and structure of numbers and patterns. Crawford shares his school's innovative, integrated approach to the teaching of this often-misunderstood subject: "Each topic in the mathematics curriculum begins with a tangible observation of the natural world, a question arising from natural philosophy, or mathematical speculation

16. Lockhart, *Mathematician's Lament*, 29.
17. St. Jerome Curriculum Group, "Educational Plan."

itself, and uses these explorations to discover skills and techniques. Following the theme set in the humanities, mathematics considers the fundamentals of numeracy, analysis, geometry, and logic in increasing complexity throughout its four years."[18]

Edward Trudeau is the Director of Planning and Institutional Research at Catholic University of America. He was a member of the original St. Jerome Academy curriculum committee and currently serves as vice chair of the St. Jerome Institute board. He has taught mathematics, logic, and philosophy to middle school, high school, and college students. He is delighted by St. Jerome Institute's breakthrough success in forming high-achieving high school students who love and appreciate the art of mathematics. While he does not expect a complete overhaul of teaching methods by the educational establishment any time soon, he is encouraged by the interest of educators—especially Catholic school leaders—who seek SJI out for advice about their mathematics programs. It is fitting that Catholic educators, who understand the beauty and order of God's created world, are on the cutting edge of the movement to reclaim young people's enthusiasm for this misunderstood art.

18. "Peter Crawford."

MUSIC

St. John Bosco said, "A school without music is like a body without a soul." Andrew Seeley, co-editor of *Classic Hymns for Catholic Schools* and author of *Golden Treasures: Comments on Classic Hymns for Catholic Schools*, agrees. He says Catholic schools should be communities of sacred song. He explains,

> We are musical beings. Music is as natural to us as laughter and tears. . . . The formative effect of music on the young can hardly be overestimated. Children need to hear music that will help them feel and express the whole range of human emotion in creative and healthy ways.
>
> But not only to hear! Making music is as natural to us as hearing it. God has built instruments into our body—our feet and hands to make rhythm, our voices to make melody and harmony. Children are naturally apt to sing and to be trained to sing. They have a ready memory for sung lyrics. The music they carry with them in their hearts will stay with them throughout the various circumstances of their lives. . . .
>
> Catholics need to learn to sing classic hymns so that the rich poetic expressions of Catholic doctrine, imagery, and passion in simple but beautiful melody and harmony will become a part of them,

and provide them with a lifetime of spiritual joy and consolation.[19]

Renewed Catholic schools embrace the teaching of music as a core academic subject—to be studied on its own and integrated into the full curriculum and life of the school—and not as an extracurricular opportunity to be added when resources allow.

Consider how Our Lady of Lourdes Catholic Classical School describes its music program on its website: "As the trend in education seeks to cut Music Department funding, Lourdes Classical is going in the opposite direction. Our curriculum puts greater emphasis on music. Students learn not only music theory, the art of performance, and the history of the great composers, but also how to connect with the depths of order and objective beauty communicated by music."[20]

Many Catholic schools require students to participate in a school choir, which is a wonderful way to enrich a student's educational experience with music.

Not all musical instruction is conducive to group learning at school. Many families supplement music classes at school with instruction at home on the piano,

19. "Why Catholic Schools Should Be Communities of Sacred Song: Interview with Dr. Andrew Seeley," Catholic School Playbook website, November 30, 2021, https://www.catholicschoolplaybook.com/post/why-catholic-schools-should-be-communities-of-sacred-song.

20. "The Arts," Our Lady of Lourdes Catholic School website, https://lourdesclassical.org/programs/the-arts/.

violin, or other instrument. Online classes provide budget-friendly options.

PHYSICAL EDUCATION

There was a time when parents understood that it is natural and good for children to play—to run around outside, climb trees, and compete against each other in sports and other games. In recent decades, however, parents have become increasingly eager to prepare their children for high-level sports play, and this has influenced the way they think about physical activity. Beginning early in life, parents sign their children up for rigorous sports skills workshops, summer camps, and travel teams. The goal is not "play" but enhanced performance. Competition is fierce. Children who spend evenings and weekends engaged in competitive sports have little time for other play at home—and they are increasingly being denied time for play at school.

Modern schools' obsession with performance— measured by academic assessments and sports teams' game records—causes administrators and teachers to neglect the importance of play for the sake of play. Today, many schools limit recess to twenty minutes a day and gym class to once or twice a week for young children, eliminating recess entirely by sixth grade. Sometimes gym class looks like every other class: instead of running around with classmates, students sit, listen, and fill out worksheets—for example, to learn parts and systems of the body.

Catholic schools that understand the need for children to move and play take a different approach. They give elementary school children two or three recesses, in addition to gym class, every day. The reduced time in the classroom does not hinder academic performance. On the contrary, students who have more time to move and play exhibit greater concentration in the classroom, which leads to increased academic performance.

Play is not the only goal of physical education. Consider the benefits to students of a physical education program that trains the "minds, hearts, and bodies" of students:

> But physical education is vital to classical education in other ways as well. Physical education offers students an opportunity to train their minds, hearts, and bodies into unified expressions of gracefulness. Accordingly, the physical education program should strive to train the minds, hearts, and bodies of the students.
>
> Students should develop concentration, self-discipline, and mental stamina through repetition, practice, and competitive play. They should come to recognize the excellence and gracefulness of beautiful physical achievements. They should also learn the rules as well as the proper techniques and strategies for playing all major sports.
>
> Students should practice sportsmanship and fair play; they should learn to win and lose with grace. They should participate in games and sports in which

they can both lead and be led, subordinating their own role to the good of the team. A spirit of healthy competition as well as an attitude of perseverance, commitment, and excellence should be the norm.

Students should participate in a variety of physical activities that promote strength, agility, coordination, speed, and endurance. They should be encouraged to form healthy living habits, which include getting the appropriate exercise, diet, and rest.[21]

Crawford, of St. Jerome Institute, embraces physical education as an essential part of his high school's approach of educating and forming the whole person. "Students are lovingly encouraged to be the best expressions of themselves in every aspect, including the body," he says. That's why not a day goes by at St. Jerome Institute without some sort of competition, often in association with gymnasium class, feast day games, or athletic field day competitions.

Schools focused on improving academic performance often make the mistake of assuming more time in the classroom (and more homework and more assessments) will increase learning, even for young children. Occasional assessments are vital for tracking student progress, but are unfortunately administered much too frequently and can even undermine the Catholic mission. Examples of the latter would include

21. St. Jerome Curriculum Group, "Educational Plan."

both the MAP (Measure of Academic Progress) tests as well as the SAT and other tests produced by the College Board, which not only censor the Catholic intellectual tradition but increasingly promote ideologies opposed to it. Fortunately, alternatives exist. Many leading Catholic schools report success with tests like ARK (Assessment of Religious Knowledge) and CLT (Classic Learning Test),[22] as well as contests such as the AMC (American Mathematics Contest). It is important to remember that joyful students are better students—and they make up a student body of happy, healthy learners. More class time, more homework, and more tests are rarely the answer.

Catholic schools would do their best if they ignored the traps that public schools have fallen into, including too many narrow electives, test-driven Advanced Placement classes, and dehumanizing screens. Instead, authentic Catholic schools are leading the way with an integrated curriculum; honors classes that introduce students to the greatest ideas and the most influential or beautiful works of literature, art, and music; and a humane classroom experience that encourages actual, in-person dialogue among students and teachers.

22. Full disclosure: Michael Ortner is an investor in the CLT.

CHAPTER 3

Teachers

THE LIFEBLOOD OF A SCHOOL

TEACHERS ARE THE LIFEBLOOD of a school. Great teachers make great schools. But what makes a great teacher? Mary Pat Donoghue offers her observations, developed over the course of decades working with great teachers at the best Catholic schools: "A great teacher knows Jesus Christ personally and this inspires a desire within the teacher to continually come to know him better, and to take seriously the obligation to shepherd his or her students into a deeper relationship with Christ. The great teacher is also intellectually curious, capable of experiencing wonder, and keenly aware of the dignity of the children in the classroom."[1]

Effective school leaders understand the importance of maintaining an excellent teaching faculty, which is

1. "Educator Interview: Mary Pat Donoghue," Catholic School Playbook website, https://www.catholicschoolplaybook.com/interview-mary-pat-donoghue.

why they take great care in the recruiting, hiring, and training of teachers. The result is a joyful learning environment with high teacher retention, strong family loyalty, and great interest by new and younger families eager to become a part of the school community.

BUILDING A CULTURE OF FRIENDSHIP

Jeffrey Presberg is headmaster of St. John the Beloved Academy, a Pre-K–8 parochial school in McLean, Virginia, that was founded in 1954. Until recently, St. John the Beloved was on the same path as many struggling schools: most teachers and parents had accepted a management approach to education that embraced systems, benchmarks, and an impatience for the complexities of the human experience. Students were bored, families were burdened by process, and administrators and teachers were obsessed with diagnosing and treating uncooperative children, especially boys. As a result, some families left for "free" schools with "better services." New families were not joining. Enrollment was plummeting.

Fr. Christopher J. Pollard, pastor of St. John the Beloved Catholic Church, knew he needed strong leadership to turn his school around. He recruited Presberg, an experienced educator and head of school who had been leading an all-boys school in Houston, Texas, to relocate to Virginia. It took Presberg less than three years to transform St. John the Beloved Academy.

Similar to other effective school leaders, Presberg sought to reclaim the Catholic identity and culture of his school. He started by focusing on the faculty. He parted ways with more than half of the original teachers who wanted to "manage" their classrooms rather than teach, and recruited and hired new teachers capable of inspiring children and spreading joy throughout the school. He now has a faculty of teachers who embrace his vision for the school. Together, they support each other as colleagues and friends as they learn and grow in their craft.

Presberg has been mindful about cultivating a culture of friendship among his faculty—because friendship, which is good and rewarding for its own sake, is also a powerful transformer of culture. He explains: "Friendship is the cornerstone of our school. It originates with the faculty; we are intentional about forming friendships with each other. It informs our pedagogy and schoolwide culture. It shapes how we relate to students and parents, cultivating a love of wisdom, liberal arts, and great conversation throughout the school community."[2]

Students, teachers, and parents enjoy being a part of a community of learners who are also friends. They help create stability for the school because they are less likely to leave prematurely and more likely to attract likeminded friends to join the community.

2. "Educator Interview: Jeffrey Presberg," Catholic School Playbook website, https://www.catholicschoolplaybook.com/interview-jeffrey-presberg.

Ali Ghaffari is the founder of Divine Mercy Academy (DMA) in Pasadena, Maryland, established in 2019. The career Navy fighter pilot turned leadership coach knew that in building up DMA, he needed to have teachers who were "all in" on the mission of the school. The kind of teachers that love the students and who the students love in return. Those who would do anything to further the school's mission of making "Saints and Scholars." He discovered these teachers in the stream of parents coming into his office looking for admission into the school for their children. He found that a sizable number of parents had a background in education and had chosen to use their skills to homeschool their children, but now were ready for their kids to experience a full five-day-a-week program. He explains,

> At Divine Mercy Academy, 80% of the faculty and staff have a child in the school. This has created a family-like atmosphere and a strong "all-in" culture. Whenever a need arises, there is always someone willing to step up and take it on. No task is too big or too small for any member of the DMA community. Combined with DMA's strong commitment to daily Mass, Rosary, Angelus, and Divine Mercy Chaplet, each member of the DMA family gets to live a full sacramental life every day with their children at the school with a community of friends. This has led to many visitors to the school noticing the palpable sense of joy emanating from the faculty, staff, and students. DMA is a school that everyone loves

coming to, and its admissions numbers bear this out. The school began with nineteen students, and in just five years, has grown to over 140 students.

EDUCATION IS FUELED BY RELATIONSHIPS

Presberg's experience cultivating a spirit of friendship at his school underscores an important truth observed by Elisabeth Sullivan: "Education is fueled by relationships." Strong relationships, originating with the faculty, make strong schools. She explains, "Teachers are guides for students to discover truth, goodness, and beauty in the world. *Schools that foster growth and friendship in their faculties have seen the payoff in enrollment, because that joy is compelling.*"[3]

Peter Crawford shares a similar insight. He says education is "first and foremost" about a "deep interpersonal formation" and that the "secret" to such formation rests in the faculty. He explains:

Teachers are the living lessons for our students. We searched high and low for those teachers whom we knew would not just be able to share expertise, but would also be able to model a love of learning, a deep humility, and a great passion for life. As impressive as each of our teachers is individually, they form

3. "Educator Interview: Elisabeth Sullivan," Catholic School Playbook website, https://www.catholicschoolplaybook.com/interview -elisabeth-sullivan.

an even more impressive community that is a true witness for our students.[4]

As Crawford notes, finding great teachers is essential to developing a strong faculty. Equally as important—especially for school leaders tasked with renewing their schools—is parting ways with weak or problematic teachers.

CONFRONTING ONE OF THE "HARDEST PARTS" OF THE JOB

When Presberg became headmaster of his school, he was delighted to discover that some teachers were enthusiastic about the changes he wanted to make; they acknowledged problems in their classrooms, wanted to learn how to better serve their students and families, and were eager to become a part of a newly energized faculty. Other teachers, however, resisted Presberg's changes; they didn't want to teach differently and Presberg didn't encourage them to stay. Approximately half of the original teachers left on their own or did not have their contracts renewed in the first two years. This gave Presberg the flexibility to hire new teachers to work alongside the remaining original teachers to help renew his school.

4. "Educator Interview: Peter Crawford," Catholic School Playbook website, https://www.catholicschoolplaybook.com/interview-peter-crawford.

Terminating the employment of weak or problematic teachers is an essential part of operating a strong school. It is also among the most challenging responsibilities for a school leader. Rosemary Vander Weele calls it "one of the hardest parts of the job—one that requires a lot of prayer."

She would know. When Vander Weele became principal of her school, her teachers were not eager to help her make the changes she proposed. A critical part of her success in renewing her school was facilitating a complete turnover of her teaching staff. She explains, "When I first came to Lourdes, the teachers resisted change. *We experienced 100% turnover of the original teaching faculty by the end of the third year.* Of the original teachers, approximately 40% chose not to return on their own and I did not renew the other approximately 60%."[5]

For more than a decade, Sullivan has helped inspire and train hundreds of Catholic school teachers to improve their craft, sometimes requiring the undoing of decades of harmful training and counterproductive practices in the classroom. She has helped bring about amazing transformations for teachers and schools. But she acknowledges that not all teachers can be retrained to be part of a successful renewal of a school. Some teachers have dispositions and tendencies that are difficult to overcome, making them a poor fit for Catholic schools. She shares, "Among those, I would list

5. "Educator Interview: Rosemary Vander Weele," Catholic School Playbook website, https://www.catholicschoolplaybook.com/interview -rosemary-vander-weele.

impatience, negativity, ego, favoritism, apathy, and a lack of diligence as particularly challenging. Among the non-negotiables that would make a teacher an improper fit for a school: any action or teaching that contradicts or undermines the Catholic, Christian mission of the school. A teacher whose heart is not in the mission is better off elsewhere, for everyone involved."[6]

School leaders who have the awareness and courage to confront staffing problems head-on are better able to help the rest of their teachers serve their students and school families.

HIRING: THE "MOST IMPORTANT MOMENT" OF A SCHOOL LEADER'S WORK

Crawford is clear about the critical role teachers play in shaping the culture of a school—which is why he calls hiring the "most important moment" of his work. He explains,

> *A school can only ever be as excellent as its faculty.* My goal in interviewing a teacher candidate is to discover if he or she will be a good addition to our community and whether they will be an excellent role model to the young men and women in his or her care. I am looking for teachers who have a capacity for wonder (*intellectus*), a deep humility, great courage, and a thirst for excellence. Different teachers may have

6. "Elisabeth Sullivan."

different teaching personalities, but all successful teachers ought to have a level of gravitas, an ability to establish order in their classroom, and a touch of stage presence. They should be strong leaders with a great capacity for charity.[7]

Andrew Shivone adds that once a good teacher has been hired, it is critical that the school community recognizes the need to make every effort to retain them. It is not enough simply to recruit good teachers; it is critical that they also stay after their first few years: "It is all too frequent that a young teacher arrives to a school with great hopes that they will be able to immediately transform the lives of their students. He quickly realizes that teaching is very difficult and learning the art of teaching will take many years. If they are not supported and developed, they become jaded and leave the profession. No organization can thrive with perpetual turnover."

There are a few keys that Shivone recommends for teacher retention:

I. **Build a Real Intellectual Community**: This can be done by having frequent in-service seminars, giving teachers a small budget to purchase books for their own intellectual pursuits, and actively engaging with teachers about serious questions in conversation.

7. "Peter Crawford."

2. **Support the Teacher in the Classroom**: "When you look at surveys about why teachers leave the professions, one of the most frequently cited reasons is that they don't feel supported. This means a number of things. First, that they are not getting the training and development they need to improve as teachers. Second, that the administration sometimes undermines them when they make disciplinary decisions. Third, that they are given workloads that are unreasonable." A school leader needs to be attentive in all these areas to avoid burnout and resentment on the part of the teacher.

3. **Teacher Pay**: This is maybe the most difficult issue in private schools but one that must be addressed. Shivone notes that "everyone knows they won't become rich as a teacher but resentment will build up if teachers feel like they are being taken for granted." School leaders must make it a priority to increase teacher pay as much as possible, even at the expense of other goods for the school.

RECRUITING AND ASSESSING POTENTIAL NEW TEACHERS

All great Catholic schools have high standards for their teachers. Equally important, they know how to recruit impressive candidates—often requiring relocation—and determine whether prospective new hires would be a good fit for their school communities.

The first step to filling a teaching vacancy is finding qualified candidates. The most popular resources to identify potential new hires include:

- **Word of mouth**: School leaders often find their best teachers through the recommendations of current teachers and parents who love their schools and have an interest in recruiting new teachers who will protect the culture.
- **Institute for Catholic Liberal Education**: ICLE offers two widely used services: (1) an Employment Opportunities Job Board allowing school leaders to post open positions, to be discovered by teachers seeking new opportunities and (2) a Résumé Portal allowing teachers to post their résumés, to be discovered by school leaders recruiting for open positions.
- **Colleges with strong liberal arts programs**: Many of the best Catholic schools have developed relationships with, and hired recent graduates of, the following colleges: Thomas Aquinas College, Wyoming Catholic College, University of Dallas, Franciscan University of Steubenville, University of Notre Dame, Ave Maria University, Hillsdale College, and the Honors Programs at

both Catholic University of America and Baylor University.

- **Catholic Resources**: Other helpful resources school leaders use include the Augustine Institute, Cardinal Newman Society, Sophia Institute, Chesterton Schools Network, Catholic Gigs, National Association of Private Catholic and Independent Schools, Handshake, and diocesan websites.

Deacon Christopher Roberts shares a helpful insight. He finds that telling his school's story throughout the year helps him find qualified teachers when he needs them: "We are constantly cultivating awareness of our mission through emails and website updates that those closest to us are eager to pass along. It makes it easier for us to recruit likeminded teachers to strengthen our faithful Catholic culture."[8]

ATTRIBUTES OF QUALITY CANDIDATES

When considering teaching candidates, effective school leaders look for great teachers who will contribute to and strengthen the culture of their schools. Consider the way four leaders describe what they look for in teaching candidates.

Michael Van Hecke looks for qualities of the Holy Family:

---

8. "Educator Interview: Deacon Christopher Roberts," Catholic School Playbook website, https://www.catholicschoolplaybook.com/interview -christopher-roberts.

I think of Jesus knowing all, enraptured by all of the beautiful attributes of God found in creation, and loving every single person—every one! Imagine a teacher who has a love and grasp of knowledge across many, many areas of knowing, and who loves children. Mary is all-loving and sacrificial, the principal component of a great teacher. One who will do the harder thing for herself because it is the better thing for the child. And then there is Joseph—humble, strong, just, chaste, prudent, faithful, etc. . . . In addition to that, Joseph was deeply knowledgeable and hardworking when it came to his craft. He was the model of "work ethic." These are traits to see in a well-rounded teacher. To add to that, who would not want a teacher that exhibits some of St. Joseph's other notable characteristics—Model of Workmen, Zealous Defender of Christ . . . and, the middle school boy's favorite, Terror of Demons.[9]

Janice Martinez similarly looks for saints—or at least, teachers who want to be saints: "When I hire a teacher, I always ask myself if I would entrust a child to this person. I have really high standards because children are sponges and they soak up everything, including

9. "Educator Interview: Michael Van Hecke," Catholic School Playbook website, https://www.catholicschoolplaybook.com/interview -michael-van-hecke.

spirit. So, my number one qualification is, 'Does this teacher want to be a saint?'"[10]

Crawford looks for attributes he ultimately wants in his own students: "A good question to ask when considering a candidate is whether this person is the sort of person you want your school's student to become. If the answer is no, then no amount of expertise or experience can make that candidate a good hire. Strong candidates must be humble, passionate, courageous, and fundamentally formable. They must be philosophically aligned with the vision of the school but also model the love for the true, the good, and the beautiful which we seek to foster in all of our students."[11]

Heidi Altman looks for supportive colleagues to help her current teachers: "We expect that new teachers will jump in with an openness to learn, share, and attain excellence in their classroom methods as well as in their other duties in the school community. We all depend on one another to give 100% to make the ship sail, and we are all expected to move an oar in the right direction. Negativity or resistance to continuous improvement doesn't work very well when a team is in full motion."[12]

10. "Educator Interview: Janice Martinez," Catholic School Playbook website, https://www.catholicschoolplaybook.com/interview-janice-martinez.

11. "Peter Crawford."

12. "Educator Interview: Heidi Altman," Catholic School Playbook website, https://www.catholicschoolplaybook.com/interview-heidi-altman.

APPLICATION AND INTERVIEW PROCESS

Effective school leaders rely on more than just résumés and reference checks when assessing teaching candidates. They get to know applicants—as teachers and as people—before making an offer to anyone to join their school faculty.

The interview is a critical part of the application process—and a practice many school leaders treat as more of a conversation than a series of formal questions to be asked and answered. School leaders hope to enjoy their time conversing with applicants. Even so, they have an important goal—to determine whether teaching candidates understand and are aligned with the philosophical outlook of the school and whether they are capable of cultivating wonder in children and contributing to the joyful, faithful culture of the school. Van Hecke relies on certain well-conceived questions to help him make these determinations, including, *"What are you reading now?"* and *"How have you handled / would you handle this following situation in a class?"*[13]

Another important part of the process is immersing applicants in the life of a school. This often involves having teaching candidates meet other faculty members, observe classes, and teach a demo lesson. Crawford has applicants receive constructive feedback during their demo lessons.

13. "Michael Van Hecke."

CREATING AN ATTRACTIVE TEACHING ENVIRONMENT

It's not enough for school leaders to identify great teachers they want to hire; those teachers must also want to teach at their schools. Effective school leaders are mindful about creating a desirable teaching environment to attract great teachers.

An important way schools get on the radar of great teachers is by valuing the teaching profession. Julian Malcolm says teachers appreciate his school's approach, which he is intentional about sharing with great teachers he wants to hire: "Teachers appreciate that we genuinely want them to teach. This is attractive because a lot of schools want teachers to focus on measurements and verifying outcomes. We don't want teachers to be John Dewey acolytes. We want them to have a fascination with the world because that is what is infectious and formative for their students."[14]

Another key selling point for teachers is the opportunity to join a supportive faculty of friends who help each other grow in their craft. Presberg says teachers want to be a part of his faculty because of the strong culture of friendship at his school: "As for what teachers are seeking, the culture with faculty is key. Our teachers are friends; their work is collaborative. There is no infighting. Our teachers have freedom and good material.

14. "Educator Interview: Julian Malcolm," Catholic School Playbook website, https://www.catholicschoolplaybook.com/interview-julian -malcolm.

They have room to succeed or fail. They know they must take initiative and responsibility for what they're doing and challenge themselves to get better."[15]

Mo Woltering has identified another critical selling point for faithful Catholic teachers: daily Mass. This was a big draw for Dina Zelden, an experienced teacher who relocated from New Orleans, Louisiana, moving down the street from Holy Family Academy in Manassas, Virginia, to be a part of the school's teaching faculty. She explains, "I've taught at other schools, both private and public. This is the first time I've had the opportunity to attend daily Mass during the school day. It's been transformational for me. There is no substitute for receiving the Eucharist and taking the time to sit in prayer and contemplation. It spiritually strengthens you for the job of teaching. It helps you be charitable with the different personalities of students and colleagues. It orients you toward Jesus, so you see Jesus in everyone around you, so you can care for them throughout the day."

Many faithfully Catholic schools have established such a strong reputation—both in their communities and nationally—that teachers seek them out, whether or not they have open teaching positions.

15. "Educator Interview: Jeffrey Presberg," Catholic School Playbook website, https://www.catholicschoolplaybook.com/interview-jeffrey-presberg.

TEACHER TRAINING AND FACULTY DEVELOPMENT

Andrew Zwerneman is president of Cana Academy, a nonprofit organization that studies, develops, and teaches the best ways for teachers to master their art. Zwerneman has nearly forty years of experience teaching and consulting in schools that emphasize classic humanities, including seventeen years as the head of a school in Virginia and two years as the head of a school in Arizona.

Zwerneman helps school leaders across the country improve their teaching faculty, leading to better learning and stronger schools. He sees three major weaknesses of teachers and teacher training at otherwise-strong classical and liberal schools:

1. Most teachers teach the way they were taught, which, at most colleges and universities, is not very good.

2. Many schools provide no training for teachers, but they think they do. Once or twice a year, they offer professional development, which includes an array of enrichment programs on academic topics or specific works; these programs are not designed to help teachers develop their skills as teachers.

3. Many schools that do provide training fail to cover two of the three major types of teaching: Socratic and coaching. That's because most

teaching in schools is didactic and when heads of school and veteran teachers train newer teachers, they tend to give talks—teaching didactically.[16]

ALL TEACHERS—EVEN SEASONED VETERANS— NEED TRAINING

Effective school leaders have an appreciation for teacher training and formation that many or most heads of modern schools lack; they understand that ongoing training for teachers at all levels is an indispensable part of operating a school. Sullivan explains, "No teacher is a finished product. Teaching is an art, not a science. Every year, every class, is filled with different individual students with unique needs and gifts. The tidy lesson plan or unit that worked beautifully last year might need some tweaking to engage this year's students. Once we get stuck in our routines, we grow stale or ineffective. Every educator should approach his or her vocation with a desire to continue growing. After all, a teacher should be a model of someone who never stops wanting to learn."[17]

Altman underscores the need for school leaders to support teachers in their professional growth: "All teachers need support, and all teachers should grow continually in their craft. Therefore, it is never assumed

16. "Educator Interview: Andrew Zwerneman," Catholic School Playbook website, https://www.catholicschoolplaybook.com/interview -andrew-zwerneman.

17. "Elisabeth Sullivan."

that I just hire and stick them in a classroom and call it 'good,' no matter what their experience. A professional is constantly seeking to perfect their methods and pedagogy—I am here to support that in all my teachers (and that is just as important as making a good hire in the first place)."[18]

Proper training requires the dedication of school resources—including not just time but also money. To bring master teachers into the school, send teachers to quality programs outside of the school, and purchase formative books, school leaders must add training as a line item in the budget. Van Hecke recommends allocating an amount for training that is equal to 33 to 50% of the salary of a full-time teacher.[19]

AVOIDING BAD TRAINING

It is important for leaders of Catholic schools— especially those attempting to renew their schools—to understand that all training is not equal. In fact, most training available for teachers today is inappropriate for faithfully Catholic schools; it is not informed by the Magisterium of the Catholic Church, is not motivated by the pursuit of truth, and lacks an understanding of the dignity owed to children in the classroom and parents as the primary educators of their children.

18. "Heidi Altman."
19. "Michael Van Hecke."

Altman warns, "One thing I have discovered is to be very wary of any of our state and national teacher training offerings and even some of our diocesan training modules that are delivered through those public/secular institutions. . . . They are so steeped in the progressive model of education. . . . Sending our teachers to those training sessions tends to just pull them in disparate directions; therefore, I just avoid them altogether and find other ways to provide what my teachers need."[20]

YEAR-ROUND TRAINING

Just as the Catholic faith informs all aspects of a faithful Catholic school's mission, so too does it shape its teacher training and formation. The most effective school leaders support and attend to their teachers' growth constantly. This is why Crawford considers himself not just headmaster of his school but also "teacher of teachers," dedicating a considerable amount of time every week to helping teachers grow in their craft.

Elements of an effective training program include:

- **Mentorship of new teachers by seasoned teachers**: Zwerneman advises that mentors should (a) be proven, effective teachers, (b) know the mission and culture of the school, (c) conduct weekly visits to the classrooms of the newer teachers, and (d)

20. "Heidi Altman."

provide practical feedback to correct what is not going well and encourage what is.[21]

- **Weekly class observations with written feedback**: Crawford says this is "the most important teacher formation" he provides for his teachers. He explains, "My goal is to visit every new teacher once a week and every experienced teacher once every two weeks. I also encourage teachers to visit my classes and give me their thoughts. The idea is to create a community of teachers who are all invested in growing and improving in the art of teaching. Regular observations and conversations about our classes help us to maintain that attitude of being lifelong students of the craft of teaching."

- **Supportive instructional coaching by school leaders and fellow teachers**: School leaders must continually encourage teachers to welcome and seek out opportunities to help each other grow in their craft. Sullivan explains, "Supportive instructional coaching can go a long way toward improving the confidence and skill of a struggling teacher. Strong school leaders promote a collegial climate where teachers frequently watch one another teach, sharing ideas and feedback in order to serve their students better. Often, this collaboration sparks a great deal of creativity and satisfaction among the faculty."[22]

---

21. "Andrew Zwerneman."
22. "Elisabeth Sullivan."

- **Weekly faculty meetings**: When run by a school leader who is careful to use teachers' time wisely, these meetings can provide important training to teachers confronting a myriad of opportunities and challenges in their classrooms throughout the year. Van Hecke uses these meetings to discuss how to bring insights of deeply formative books into their school. Favorite works include:
  - *Renewing Catholic Schools: How to Regain a Catholic Vision in a Secular Age*, edited by R. Jared Staudt
  - *The Heart of Culture: A Brief History of Western Education* by the Habiger Institute for Catholic Leadership
  - *The Art of Teaching* by Gilbert Highet
  - *The Seven Laws of Teaching* by John Milton Gregory
  - *The Holy See's Teaching on Catholic Schools* by Archbishop J. Michael Miller
- **Monthly and summer training**: Schools that take training seriously provide monthly and summer training, often bringing in master teachers from the Institute for Catholic Liberal Education and Cana Academy, or utilizing resources from the Augustine Institute, Sophia Teachers, Chesterton Schools Network, Classical Academic Press, Circe Institute, Denver Catholic Biblical School, Franciscan at Home, Memoria Press, Singapore Math, and other groups. Vander Weele uses this time to unite her faculty around her school's mission

"to form disciples of Jesus Christ." She explains, "I try to start with more theoretical training and then drill down to the practical. Most teachers want the practical of what they need to do in their classrooms. I understand. I'm a type A personality myself. But we never jump to practical training without first spending time considering the souls entrusted to us and the human and formative elements of what we're doing."[23]

- **Semi-annual reviews**: Zwerneman advises that school leaders meet with teachers twice a year to identify gaps, devise tactics to close gaps, and develop a follow-up evaluation process to determine whether gaps have been closed.
- **Boot camp for new teachers**: Zwerneman recommends that school leaders host a week-long (or longer) boot camp for new teachers during their first three years. Boot camps should take place in the summer, well in advance of school so that mundane matters (for example, mapping out lesson plans, doing the readings or the problem sets, practicing the labs, doing the translations, etc.) can be peacefully attended to. Boot camps should include the following elements:
  - ♦ **Formal presentations**: School leaders should give formal presentations examining the content of the school's mission and its culture. Mission is what the school is established to

---

23. "Rosemary Vander Weele."

accomplish: what impact the school hopes to have on which population. Culture consists of the most important practices by which the school is a community of learning devoted to its mission. Teachers need to be trained to be keepers and practitioners of the culture.

♦ **Modeling**: Seasoned veteran teachers need to model good teaching: what to teach (curricular content) and how to teach it (pedagogy). They need to model in ways that point out the best strategies to follow, clarify the pitfalls to avoid, and demonstrate key maneuvers that constitute the most effective means to move students from one proficiency level to the next. Danny Flynn, principal of St. Jerome Academy, has found great value in this approach, which he says has "shortened the learning curve" for new teachers.

♦ **New teacher practice**: New teachers should lead exercises that are evaluated by the veterans. Veterans should provide coaching feedback and provide multiple opportunities for new teachers to try again, improve, and demonstrate proficiency.

MODELS OF SERVANT LEADERSHIP

The most effective leaders of Catholic schools are servant leaders, modeled after Jesus Christ's sacrificial love in service of God's children. They model servant leadership to their teachers, who in turn model it to each other and their students. Parents at great Catholic schools often note that the mentorship teachers provide for their children—which is based in significant part on teachers' modeling of virtuous behavior—is among the greatest blessings of being a part of the school community.

Nicholas and Maruska Healy are parents at the St. Jerome Institute. They are "deeply impressed" with SJI teachers who are "living their faith and sharing their love for Christ with the students." They explain,

> All of the teachers seem to be aware of the overall vision of the school. They seem to understand how the whole curriculum fits together and are capable and willing to help each other; if need be, they can teach each other's subjects. *This is a rare gift—an experience found similarly in a family where people naturally need to help one another.* The teachers spend lots of time with the students as well, during lunch breaks, or after school, offering help and encouragement. It is good to have role models for our son.[24]

24. "Parent Interview: Nicholas and Maruska Healy," Catholic School Playbook website, https://www.catholicschoolplaybook.com/interview-nicholas-maruska-healy.

School leaders have many demands on their time. The success of the schools highlighted in this playbook suggest that attending to teacher training and formation is among the most important.

CHAPTER 4

Families

THE PRIMARY EDUCATORS OF CHILDREN

A COMMON THEME among thriving Catholic schools is a deep respect for parents as the primary educators of their children. While many, perhaps all, Catholic schools include this Church teaching in their mission statement or school handbook, faithful schools pay more than lip service to this principle, establishing relationships with families that are true partnerships grounded in the Catholic faith. The result is a school community where the school serves parents, not the other way around, and teachers and families work together to form students in Christ.

PARTNERSHIP

The Church's teaching on the proper role of a school in relation to families and the Church—as set forth by Pope Pius XI in the encyclical *Divini Illius Magistri* nearly one hundred years ago—is a best practice of Catholic schools today. Pope Pius XI wrote, "The school is by its very nature an institution subsidiary and complementary to the family and to the Church. It follows logically and necessarily that it must not be in opposition to, but in positive accord with, those other two elements, and form with them a perfect moral union, constituting one sanctuary of education, as it were, with the family and the Church."[1]

What Pope Pius XI referred to as a "perfect moral union" is what today's school leaders and parents call a "partnership." Mo Woltering explains,

> The mission of Holy Family Academy is: "To assist families by providing Catholic education that is faithful to the Magisterium of the Church through a classical curriculum in an environment that is thoroughly Catholic." Every part of this mission statement is important, but the first part is often overlooked. We are serious about our partnership with parents. We welcome their participation at school, but more importantly, we want them to be active at home. *We need parents to be thoughtful and intentional about the structure of their home life so that their children can thrive at school.*[2]

1. Pius XI, *Divini Illius Magistri* 77, encyclical letter, December 31, 1929, vatican.va.

2. "Educator Interview: Mo Woltering," Catholic School Playbook website, https://www.catholicschoolplaybook.com/interview-mo-woltering.

Heidi Altman is "constantly seeking" ways to strengthen her partnership with parents. She explains, "I am finding that more and more parents truly need a partner that will teach them the beauty of our faith and how to live it out in the domestic church (their homes). As a school, we are constantly seeking even more ways to provide support to parents and model to them how to raise their children counterculturally and how to be strong in the truths of their faith. Strong families produce strong children, and strong children grow up to establish more strong families!"[3]

Abby Sandel credits her partnership with her school with helping to prepare her children for "a meaningful life." She says, "I believe that St. Jerome's classical curriculum isn't just the best possible educational foundation for my children. It's also the best preparation for a meaningful life. *I can't imagine raising my children without the support and partnership of the faculty at SJA and the community that surrounds it.*"[4]

Effective school leaders know that the strength of a school community depends on the makeup of its families—and because new families join the school community every year, admissions and parental education and involvement must always be a top priority.

---

3. "Educator Interview: Heidi Altman," Catholic School Playbook website, https://www.catholicschoolplaybook.com/interview-heidi-altman.

4. "Parent Interview: Abby Sandel," Catholic School Playbook website, https://www.catholicschoolplaybook.com/interview-abby-sandel.

ADMISSIONS

Most schools require the following basic steps in the admissions process:

1. Application form
2. Transcripts
3. Referrals

Schools that take extra steps to collect more information about families are able to make better admissions decisions.

FAMILY INTERVIEWS

School leaders who take a personal interest in getting to know families are in the best position to cultivate and protect a positive school culture. That's why the most effective leaders prioritize face-to-face meetings as a critical part of the application process. There is simply no better way to draw out the values and priorities of families seeking to be a part of a school community than by spending time in conversation. Peter Crawford explains,

> Significant conversation is entailed in the application and enrollment of a new student. *We are looking for families that earnestly care about their child's character and want him or her to grow.* We want the majority of our families to be practicing Catholics and to

support and understand the traditional form of education we offer, which is gravitated by a pursuit of the true, the good, and the beautiful. While there may be many differences between our families, we want all of them to be community minded, to understand education as a formation in reality, and to support the meaningful challenges we offer their children and share in our final desire for their child: sanctity.[5]

Interviewing is a skill that must be developed. The best interviewers are experienced listeners who pay attention to what parents say, how they say it, and what questions they ask; they are intentional about asking thoughtful questions designed to encourage parents to be candid about their values and culture at home.

Cyril Cruz is principal of Holy Innocents Parish School, a TK (transitional kindergarten)–8 parochial school in Long Beach, California, that offers families "an education rooted in the Catholic classical liberal arts tradition." She has developed a list of four questions that she always asks while getting to know families during the interview process. They are:

1. Why do you want your child to be formed at our school?
2. How do you practice your faith?

5. "Educator Interview: Peter Crawford," Catholic School Playbook website, https://www.catholicschoolplaybook.com/interview-peter-crawford.

3. Describe your family life. (Probe about discipline, schedule, etc.)
4. What is your philosophy on technology?[6]

Julian Malcolm finds it helpful to interview students and parents separately. He explains,

It is sometimes the case that parents are the ones pushing a resistant kid into a Christian education, especially in high school. That isn't necessarily a deal-killer, but it does need to be addressed. It is always the case that we want to hear what prospective students think about school. What is their attitude about learning? Are they able to verbalize an answer or are they used to having their parents speak for them? Leaning too much on mom and dad to answer those questions can sometimes deprive a young person of an age-appropriate independence. It's okay if the interview is the first time they have had to give an account of their position on school, but it does need to happen.

Likewise, we sometimes get a more clear picture from parents when it is just adults talking. We want to know what it is they want for their children. It may seem like an obvious question, but it is often the case that the interview process may be the first time

6. "Educator Interview: Cyril Cruz," Catholic School Playbook website, https://www.catholicschoolplaybook.com/interview-cyril-cruz.

a couple is invited to articulate their desires for their children. It is simple, but high impact.

All school leaders have different styles, but they all share the same goal: to determine whether a family shares the values of the school community and will contribute positively to the overall culture of the school. "On a basic level," Woltering explains, this means identifying families whose highest priority is "getting their kids to heaven and understanding that this requires opting out of mainstream culture to a large extent."

READING ASSIGNMENTS

The Catholic liberal education movement has gained considerable momentum in recent years. Even so, most parents today—including many who seek out faithfully Catholic schools—lack a concrete understanding of the philosophical and practical differences of schools steeped in the educational heritage of the Church.

An effective way to help familiarize prospective families on their approach is by assigning reading as they move through the application process. An ideal book for parents is *Renewing Catholic Schools: How to Regain a Catholic Vision for a Secular Age* by the Institute for Catholic Liberal Education. Other helpful books include *An Introduction to Classical Education: A Guide for Parents* by Christopher Perrin and *The Lost Tools of Learning* by Dorothy Sayers.

Altman says giving parents books to read during the application process allows them to "all . . . begin speaking the same language." She explains, "I have found that as long as we are truthful and clear in our conversations with parents about our mission, our model, and our expectations of students and families, then it is easy to determine whether or not parents are the right 'fit' for our school. Though I believe *all* families *can* be the right 'fit,' I know that not every family is ready to engage fully in the model of education that we offer."[7]

Altman says another benefit of discussing assigned reading is that it gives her a head start in knowing how best to serve families; having substantive conversations helps her know where parents will need support if their children are admitted to, and enroll in, her school.

SHADOW DAY

Shadow days are an increasingly popular part of the application process for many Catholic schools because they give schools and families the opportunity to evaluate each other in a natural setting.

Shadow days are days set aside by schools during which prospective students "shadow" current students during a normal school day. Over the course of several hours, prospective students participate in classes and interact with students and teachers. The experience allows prospective students to make observations

7. "Heidi Altman."

about the school and envision themselves as a member of the student body. It also allows teachers to observe prospective students and provide feedback to administrators making admissions decisions. Malcolm explains why he makes shadow days the first step in his school's application process:

> Students immediately recognize that our classrooms are different. They see that everything about the classroom experience communicates that students are worthy of respect. Teachers treat students as young people on their way to adulthood. Students discuss their work together during and in between classes; they are interested in the material and in each other's ideas and contributions to the academic life of the school. *How prospective students respond to that experience tells us a lot about whether or not they are ready and a good fit for the school.*[8]

RECRUITING

Recruiting—the process of finding new families to join a school community—is critical to the continued operation of a school. Schools that fail to recruit suffer decreased enrollment, decreased tuition revenue, budget cuts, and, ultimately, closure. Schools with

8. "Educator Interview: Julian Malcolm," Catholic School Playbook website, https://www.catholicschoolplaybook.com/interview-julian-malcolm.

happy families—especially those with an established track record of excellence—rely on word of mouth more than any other form of recruiting. Michael Van Hecke explains, "For 15 years we have not recruited. We built a strong, mission-imbued school, especially through our admissions and hiring, and word of mouth has kept it full. This is so strong that, on average, every year we have one family move from across or out of state in order to be near to our school so they can become part of it."[9]

But no school starts with full enrollment. Start-up and transitioning schools need to recruit—quickly and efficiently—to bring in tuition revenue to pay teachers and cover other costs.

PARETO PRINCIPLE

The most successful schools are those that apply the 80/20 rule, also known as the Pareto Principle, to recruiting efforts. The 80/20 rule states that 80% of the results come from 20% of the action. Assuming that approximately 20% of Catholics take their faith seriously (recent polls support this), Catholic schools should focus recruiting efforts on this 20%, rather than allocating equal resources on lukewarm Catholics.[10] It is critical

9. "Educator Interview: Michael Van Hecke," Catholic School Playbook website, https://www.catholicschoolplaybook.com/interview-michael-van-hecke.

10. "Poll: Young Adults More Likely than Older Catholics to Accept All of Church Teaching," Catholic News Agency website, October 20, 2020, https://www.catholicnewsagency.com/news/46290/poll-young-adults-more-likely-than-older-catholics-to-accept-all-of-church-teaching.

that new and transitioning schools get the right kind of families—those who will support and strengthen the culture the school is trying to develop—in the door first.

In practice, this means:

- Identifying the more devout Catholic parishes, publications, homeschooling families and co-ops, and schools (K–8 schools are excellent resources for high schools);
- Developing relationships with pastors, religious education directors, reporters and editors, heads of schools, and other influential members of the community;
- Speaking after Mass, publishing notices in church bulletins, posting information on Listservs and in social media groups, advertising in Catholic publications and on social media, and having articles written about the school in Catholic publications, with the goal of having families visit the school, which, Crawford emphasizes, is "more convincing than any article or talk";
- Hosting events at the school, at the homes of faithful Catholics in the community, and at the meeting places of well-respected Catholic groups.

It also means enlisting the help of the 20% of current families who are most enthusiastic about their school and who have strong relationships with other local Catholic families in the community.

ENRICHMENT CLASSES FOR HOMESCHOOL
FAMILIES

Fr. Robert Sirico notes that some pastors see home-schooling families as competition for Catholic schools. When he became pastor of his parish, he rejected this approach as unpastoral and unwise. In keeping with his vision of the school as an apostolate of the parish, he offered enrichment classes for homeschoolers in Latin, mathematics, and science, charging half the full-time tuition. The classes were a huge success. They supported homeschooling parents, provided extra revenue for the school, and built relationships between homeschooling families and the school that resulted in many home-schooled children enrolling at the school. Because of the enrichment classes, homeschool families accounted for the largest growth in new student admissions.

INTEGRATING PARENTS INTO THE LIFE
OF THE SCHOOL

Integrating parents into the life of a school looks different for faithful Catholic schools than it does for secular and most Catholic schools. That's because Catholic schools exist to serve families, not the other way around; they partner with families to prepare children for a life of faith and virtue, with the goal of fulfilling God's plan to spend eternity with him in heaven. They understand that the most important formation happens at home under the guidance of well-formed parents.

Effective school leaders involve parents in school activities in a way that does not interfere with family life. They also support them in their vocation as parents in three important ways: (1) by helping parents grow in their faith, (2) by helping parents become lifelong learners, and (3) by helping parents navigate the challenges of raising faithful children in our modern, secular society.

PARENTAL INVOLVEMENT IN SCHOOL ACTIVITIES

Families form bonds that strengthen the whole school community when they spend time together in a social or volunteer capacity. Effective school leaders welcome parental involvement and express their gratitude for volunteers, without placing an undue burden on family life. Rosemary Vander Weele shares her approach: "We do ask that every family does twenty-five volunteer hours, but we don't track it closely. If the reality of a family's situation is that lunch is right in the middle of naptime, I'm not going to force a mother to bring her three little ones in during naptime and then have them suffer or get a babysitter."[11]

Many schools—especially small schools and schools with low tuition revenue—rely heavily on volunteers to carry out day-to-day operations, including overseeing lunch and recess, assisting teachers with administrative

11. "Educator Interview: Rosemary Vander Weele," Catholic School Playbook website, https://www.catholicschoolplaybook.com/interview-rosemary-vander-weele.

tasks, and coaching sports teams. Many also use parent volunteers to help with special projects—for example, painting classroom walls, building a playground, or planting flowers—and special events, including field trips and fundraisers (see chapter five for more information about fundraising).

Maintaining a well-run volunteer program takes planning and effort. Cultivating strong relationships with parent volunteers is key—as is choosing the right parents to fill certain roles. Parents who are notably positive, friendly, and thoughtful should be sought out for roles involving significant interaction with other members of the school community. Parents who are susceptible to negativity and complaining are better suited for behind-the-scenes roles.

HELPING PARENTS GROW IN FAITH

Robin Fisher is principal of St. Regis Academy, a once-struggling Pre-K–8 parochial school in Kansas City, Missouri. She renewed her school by embracing Catholic liberal education in 2018. From the start, she has been intentional about supporting parents in their faith formation. "Parents must have a relationship with Christ and must be models of this for their children," she explains. That's why, to support parents in strengthening their faith, she recommends parents take advantage of the Mass above all else.

The Mass is the central act of worship for Catholics. It is where one encounters the Eucharist—the source and summit of the Christian life—and receives special graces. As St. Padre Pio is credited with saying, "Every holy Mass, heard with devotion, produces in our souls marvelous effects, abundant spiritual and material graces which we, ourselves, do not know."

A beautiful tradition among many Catholic schools is allowing parents to sit with their children at school Masses. Children feel special when their parents spend time with them during the school day, and there is no better activity around which to strengthen family bonds and model devotion to Christ than the holy Mass.

In addition to promoting the Mass, many Catholic schools encourage parents to utilize a multitude of popular resources to cultivate faith formation at home, including:

- Augustine Institute (especially FORMED)
- Word on Fire
- TAN Books
- Sophia Institute Press
- Loyola Press
- New Advent
- Pontifical John Paul II Institute
- Trinity House Community

In addition, schools encourage parents to take advantage of resources at their parish, including youth ministry, Amazing Parish, ENDOW for women, and That Man Is You! for men.

HELPING PARENTS BECOME LIFELONG LEARNERS

Chapter 2 explores the importance of teachers modeling a love of learning in order to inspire wonder in their students. As Elisabeth Sullivan explains, "Teachers cannot give what they do not have."[12] The same is true—and to a greater extent—for parents, who are the primary educators of their children.

Deacon Christopher Roberts shares an analogy explaining why it's important for a child's intellectual and spiritual life to be cultivated at home: "If you eat three nutritious meals a day and then go down to the kitchen every night and eat junk food, your diet will not be successful. Similarly, if parents send children to a classical school for eight hours a day, but their home life is dominated by technology and media, with no prayer, the classical education will not be successful."[13]

In addition to encouraging parents to learn what their children are learning at home (Danny Flynn tells parents that homework is "a game the whole family can play"[14]), effective school leaders are proactive about hosting special educational events for parents. Many

---

12. "Educator Interview: Elisabeth Sullivan," Catholic School Playbook website, https://www.catholicschoolplaybook.com/interview-elisabeth-sullivan.

13. "Educator Interview: Deacon Christopher Roberts," Catholic School Playbook website, https://www.catholicschoolplaybook.com/interview-christopher-roberts.

14. "Educator Interview: Danny Flynn," Catholic School Playbook website, https://www.catholicschoolplaybook.com/interview-danny-flynn.

schools give parents the opportunity to gather to hear from guest speakers and participate in seminars on select works, for example, "The Gettysburg Address" or the fairy tale "Cinderella." St. Jerome Institute has hosted events exploring topics including "Liberal Education and Social Crisis" and "Tradition and Religious Art." Father Pollard hosts book seminars on classics such as Augustine's *City of God* for adults at St. John the Beloved as another way for them to continue to grow in faith and intellect. Imagine the impact on our culture if pastors and school leaders regularly worked together to run seminars on classic texts for parents and other adults in their communities!

HELPING PARENTS NAVIGATE THE CHALLENGES OF MODERN SECULAR SOCIETY

Harmful societal influences can sabotage the efforts of well-meaning parents trying to raise virtuous children. A growing body of research is showing how video games (particularly for boys), social media (particularly for girls), and the use of smartphones in general have become an assault on the innocence, mental health, and sense of wonder of children. Experienced school leaders often see a myriad of parenting approaches play out over the course of many years; they are in an ideal position to offer wisdom to parents who are encountering challenges for the first time. Effective school leaders embrace the opportunity to support parents in this critical way, and can be catalysts for creating a positive alternative community that rejects the secular, screen-obsessed mainstream culture.

Vander Weele says she "works very hard" to alert parents to the dangers facing their children in the modern world. She speaks with parents and organizes book studies exploring timely topics. Recently, she felt so strongly about helping parents benefit from Dr. Leonard Sax's *The Collapse of Parenting* that she bought a copy for every family at her school. She explains, "Parenting is going down the gutter very quickly. We are over-diagnosing kids and allowing harm to happen to them because we aren't parenting well. I want parents to realize how critical their role is."[15]

Other books recommended by Vander Weele and other leaders of Catholic schools include:

- Dr. Nicholas Kardaras, *Glow Kids: How Screen Addiction is Hijacking Our Kids—and How to Break the Trance*
- Neil Postman, *Technopoly: The Surrender of Culture to Technology*
- Cal Newport, *Digital Minimalism: Choosing a Focused Life in a Noisy World*
- Meg Meeker, *Hero: Being the Strong Father Your Children Need* and *Strong Mothers, Strong Sons*
- Ben Sasse, *The Vanishing American Adult: Our Coming-of-Age Crisis and How to Rebuild a Culture of Self-Reliance*

15. "Rosemary Vander Weele."

- Dr. Anthony Esolen, *Out of the Ashes: Rebuilding American Culture*
- Josef Pieper, *Only the Lover Sings: Art and Contemplation*
- John Taylor Gatto, *Dumbing Us Down: The Hidden Curriculum of Compulsory Schooling*
- *Mother Love: A Manual For Christian Mothers* (Angelus Press)

Online courses that help parents in the formation of their children, such as "Fathers and Sons" from Forge, are also a worthwhile resource for Catholic schools to share with their families.[16]

WELCOMING CHILDREN WITH DISABILITIES

In *The Holy See's Teaching on Catholic Schools,* Archbishop J. Michael Miller instructed that Catholic schools—which he described as "an indispensable instrument in carrying out the Church's mission"—should complement "the primary role of parents in educating their children" and be "available to all."[17]

Founded in 2010 to meet the "great need for high-quality Catholic education that could serve typical children and children with special needs alike," Immaculata

16. "Fathers and Sons: Conversations on Sex Ed, Marriage, and Masculinity," Forge website, https://courses.myforge.org/courses/fathersandsons.

17. Archbishop J. Michael Miller, *The Holy See's Teaching on Catholic Schools* (Manchester, NH: Sophia Institute Press, 2006), 61.

is a Pre-K–12 independent Catholic school that is officially recognized by the Archdiocese of Louisville. The school utilizes a classical liberal arts curriculum to provide an "unapologetically" Catholic education "for the whole family." The school accepts children with various special needs but places a special emphasis on Down syndrome.

Special needs children represent approximately 15% of the total student body (generally one to two children in each classroom). The formula benefits all students as they point out on their website: "This arrangement does not detract from our rigorous classical curriculum—on the contrary, it enhances it! Integration benefits both typically and specially developing children, who would in all likelihood be otherwise deprived of the opportunity to interact with each other. We find that our philosophy of inclusion perfectly complements the goals of a truly classical education, whose end is the development not only of the intellect but the entire human person."[18]

Catholics with special needs have a strong ally in Bishop Michael Burbidge of Arlington, Virginia. His goal is to help every school and parish in the Arlington diocese offer special education and inclusion programs. He is making significant progress toward this goal with nearly half of the forty-one diocesan schools having such an initiative.

---

18. "Whole Person, Whole Family," Immaculata Classical Academy website, https://immaculata.org/inclusive-education.

CHAPTER 5

Building Community

A LIVING ENCOUNTER WITH A CULTURAL
INHERITANCE

MICHAEL VAN HECKE was a pioneer in the movement
to renew Catholic education. Having served as a Catholic educator and headmaster, he helped organize the first
gatherings of independent Catholic schools beginning
in 1993 and helped found St. Augustine Academy in
1994. To answer the growing need for sound curricular
materials and genuine teacher formation based on a
proper Christian anthropology (an understanding of
humanity from a Christian perspective), he founded the
Institute for Catholic Liberal Education in 1999. He has
been inspiring and training Catholic school leaders and
educators to transform their school communities ever
since.

Van Hecke is one of a handful of experienced Catholic educators featured in the compelling book *Renewing
Catholic Schools: How to Regain a Catholic Vision in a*

Secular Age. He shares a profound insight about school communities: "We need to think of schools less as institutions, and more as communities. For a community is communal, human, a place where culture exists and formation occurs. As the Church teaches, a school is 'a privileged place in which, through a living encounter with a cultural inheritance, cultural formation occurs.'"[1]

Effective school leaders build community by fostering friendships among faculty, families, and students, reinforcing shared values through regular school communications, and establishing customs that bond members of the community to each other.

FOSTERING FRIENDSHIPS

One of the most important ways Van Hecke builds community at his school is by "intentionally working on becoming friends to all." His school is intentional about "communicating and being present," especially at social events and everyday activities, including the carpool line.[2]

Being present to foster friendships is an approach that resonates with Peter Crawford. He says a school leader "should be superabundantly present" to faculty,

1. Michael Van Hecke, "Forming a School Community," in *Renewing Catholic Schools: How to Regain a Catholic Vision in a Secular Age*, ed. R. Jared Staudt (Washington, DC: Catholic Education Press, 2020), 96.

2. "Educator Interview: Michael Van Hecke," Catholic School Playbook website, https://www.catholicschoolplaybook.com/interview-michael-van-hecke.

students, and parents because "a school is fundamentally a community before it is a model or a curriculum." He explains,

> The health and sense of community of the school flows from the faculty. . . . A good headmaster makes time every day to be a presence in the faculty office, to share a sense of humor with the teachers and to be available to their cares and concerns. School community entails a shared vision, so it is important that all the teachers are actively and consistently informed by the SJI vision in their interactions with students, parents, and each other. This sort of unity requires headmaster presence.
>
> Likewise, a headmaster must be present to the students. . . . I make it a point to greet every student every day, and I regularly meet with students during the school day, often as mentor but just as likely in a friendly and casual manner. . . . Important formative moments include our occasional assemblies, when I speak to students in a more formal and elevated capacity.
>
> Parents are most difficult to interact with personally on a regular basis because they do not attend school. It is a good practice, therefore, for a headmaster to be present during drop-off and pick-up as this is, sadly enough, the significant firsthand experience parents have of the school. Aside from this time, a

headmaster should be present at events and make it a point to interact with parents.[3]

COMMUNICATIONS WITH SCHOOL FAMILIES

Heidi Altman is mindful that many of her school families live too far away to spend a considerable amount of time on school grounds. "Therefore, we do intentionally build and strengthen our school community in order to ensure that the family who travels forty-five miles to school is just as connected as the family who walks their child across the street to our campus," she says.[4]

One of the most effective ways to build community—even with families who do not spend a considerable amount of time on campus—is by coordinating a weekly communication that families look forward to reading. Altman's weekly communication, which she sends to current school families, as well as faculty, alumni, and donors, is called the *Ram Report*, after its school mascot.

Van Hecke's weekly communication is called *The Blue Letter*. He shares how being intentional with his weekly messaging has strengthened his school community and enculturated new families for more than thirty years:

3. "Educator Interview: Peter Crawford," Catholic School Playbook website, https://www.catholicschoolplaybook.com/interview-peter-crawford.
4. "Educator Interview: Heidi Altman," Catholic School Playbook website, https://www.catholicschoolplaybook.com/interview-heidi-altman.

One of the most effective communication tools I have used for over thirty years is a weekly letter. Early on, that letter was sent on blue paper to make it distinguishable from the school announcements. Thirty years later, it is still called "The Blue Letter." Generally, the front features a letter from the headmaster (or a "guest column" by a teacher) and the back contains announcements, calendar events, and the like. The front side may contain a teaching, an article excerpt, a poem or quote, or even a recounting of something from the school Mass or a class.

Over many years, with thirty or more of these letters each year, *we start to convey a vocabulary (e.g., truth, beauty, and goodness), a culture, a conversation, and a philosophy that undergirds the nature of our school community.* It provides a base for us all to think about and discuss. This, in turn, helps enculturate new families into the life of the school and the long-developed intellectual traditions of the school.[5]

Danny Flynn communicates with families through a weekly newsletter called *The Vox*. Once a month, *The Vox* features a monthly bulletin—called the *Domestic Church Bulletin*—that is created by parents and reviewed by the school administration. The *Domestic Church Bulletin* includes devotions, prayers, traditions, a saint study, recipes, and opportunities for pilgrimages. Flynn describes it as "a wonderful resource for families to be

5. "Michael Van Hecke."

able to celebrate the liturgical calendar with various traditions right in their own home," thus bonding school families to one another through participation in shared experiences.[6]

Mo Woltering sends a weekly email to share important messages and upcoming events with his school community. The highlight every week is Woltering's opening commentary, which school parent Holly Smith describes as "always relevant, whether addressing current events, Church matters, or raising faithful families." Smith says Woltering's insights are "so on point" that she often sends them to likeminded friends.

Julian Malcolm includes links to articles exploring Catholicism, education, and parenting in his weekly email. The Institute for Catholic Liberal Education is a favorite source for articles aimed at assisting parents in their capacity as primary educators of their children. When Malcolm had an article, titled "Forming Resilient Teenagers," published in an online magazine for Catholic psychology, he used his weekly newsletter to share it with families and to build consensus around the school's educational philosophy.

In addition to sharing weekly newsletters, many Catholic schools use Facebook to share school news and build community. Some also use Instagram and YouTube.

---

6. "Educator Interview: Danny Flynn," Catholic School Playbook website, https://www.catholicschoolplaybook.com/interview-danny-flynn.

The headmaster of Sacred Heart Academy holds a weekly video conference open to all school families and staff to provide an update on school activities and priorities.

ESTABLISHING UNIQUE CUSTOMS

One of the most energizing ways effective school leaders build community is by creating customs unique to their school that reinforce the culture of their school. Customs give a school community the opportunity to anticipate and appreciate a particular activity or practice—for example, a special prayer or seasonal event—that distinguishes the school and bonds members of the community to one another.

Consider the unique customs of some of the schools highlighted in this playbook:

- Martin Saints Classical High School holds Frassati Fridays, where students alternate between an outdoor adventure (hiking, canoeing), cultural excursions (art museum, ballet, orchestra, opera), and a corporal work of mercy (serving meals and praying with the homeless, visiting an old folks' home).
- St. Augustine Academy hosts an annual Classics Day, a day-long celebration of speeches, banquets, and competitions—identified with different countries, clans, or groups from ancient, medieval, or

American history—involving all K–12 students and faculty.

- St. Jerome Institute hosts a monthly liturgical feast celebration with competitive "games of renown," live music, and feasting.
- St. John the Beloved Academy hosts House Festival Days, "where students, faculty, and staff attend Mass, enjoy a dress-down day, a special schoolwide lunch, and partake in games and poetry recitation competitions" amongst the school's four houses.[7]
- Holy Child Catholic School hosts a Fairy Tale Friday every fall, where students translate parts of a Grimms' Fairy Tale or other story and act it out.
- St. Jerome Academy hosts a Carpe Noctem Christmas craft fair and Christmas concert with a living nativity.
- The Summit Academy holds two overnight outdoor retreats where students have the opportunity to gain new experiences and develop skills in a safe but challenging environment.
- Holy Family Academy focuses on the dignity of the human person and the right to life every January by praying for an end to legalized abortion at Mass, holding a pro-life essay contest where winners read their reports in front of the whole school, and creating posters to carry at the annual March for Life in Washington, DC.

---

7. "House System," Saint John the Beloved Academy website, accessed June 12, 2024, https://stjohnacademy.org/student-life/house-system/.

CHAPTER 6

Finances

THE BUSINESS OF OPERATING A
SUSTAINABLE SCHOOL

CATHOLIC SCHOOLS ARE PRIVATE, non-profit organizations that rely on voluntary support to keep their doors open. For Catholic schools to survive, their revenue must meet their expenses. This means, first and foremost, that they must provide a quality education that parents are willing to pay for and is significantly better than the "free" education offered by public schools. In addition, Catholic schools must set tuition at a level that will cover a considerable portion of operational costs, without pricing local families out of the school. They must also develop an effective fundraising program to bridge the gap between tuition revenue and costs.

Making the numbers work year after year is a daunting task. In fact, it is the aspect of operating a school that many leaders of Catholic schools identify as their greatest challenge.

All school communities are different. The precise calculations for tuition and financial aid that work for one school may not be a good fit for another school. Similarly, a specific fundraising initiative that succeeds at one school may fail to raise money at another school. Even so, it is instructive to consider how the most effective school leaders approach their finances; many have developed ideas and practices that should be adopted as best practices and sources of inspiration for emerging schools.

TUITION AND FINANCIAL ASSISTANCE

A commitment to making tuition affordable for families—by setting tuition low and/or offering generous financial aid and sibling discounts—is a hallmark of faithful Catholic schools.

Mary Pat Donoghue says accessibility is "critical" to the mission of Catholic schools. She shares the ideal approach of schools committed to advancing this mission: "Ideally, schools would offer a 'full cost, full need' tuition model. This means, first, establishing the actual cost per student. Secondly, the school would undertake a process to determine family need (for example, financial aid applications)."[1]

Accessibility is critical to the mission of Catholic schools, so certainly sibling discounts and financial aid

1. "Educator Interview: Mary Pat Donoghue," Catholic School Playbook website, https://www.catholicschoolplaybook.com/interview-mary-pat-donoghue.

should be made available. But it's important for everyone involved to know and understand the financial needs of the school: paying teachers a decent wage is important and will contribute to the school's stability. We applaud schools that set up tuition assistance funds and encourage parishioners and grandparents to contribute.

The three most common tuition models are:

- **Affordability Model**: Low tuition, plus modest sibling discounts, plus moderate financial aid
- **Family Model**: Low tuition, plus significant sibling discounts, plus modest-to-moderate financial aid
- **Competitive Model**: Higher tuition, plus no-to-modest sibling discounts, plus modest-to-significant financial aid

AFFORDABILITY MODEL

Keeping tuition low is a priority for Heidi Altman because she wants all families—including those of modest means—to be able to access "an education centered on faith, virtue, wisdom, and apostleship." She accomplishes this goal by offering sibling discounts in addition to financial aid. Her school provides aid to 30% to 40% of its families, with an average grant of $1,000. She explains, "As a pro-life Catholic school, we are committed to keeping tuition low for our families while providing an exemplary education program for all. A Catholic school education is the best investment for a child's faith formation, academics, and happiness, and we are glad to share in the financial sacrifice by providing tuition discounts, engaging with our families in rigorous fundraising, offering needs-based tuition scholarships, and partnering with St. Mary of the Assumption Parish to fund our program."[2]

Cyril Cruz uses a similar model. Her school offers low tuition with sibling discounts and financial aid. 60% of families, representing 70% of all students, receive financial assistance. The average grant amount is $3,689.[3]

Rosemary Vander Weele also embraces the affordability model. Most of her school families live on a single income and appreciate the low tuition and sibling discounts. 50% of her school families receive financial aid. She is sensitive to the financial concerns of families even as she promotes the high value of her program. She explains,

> I struggle with our low tuition because I don't want to undersell us. There's something to be said about parents embracing the fact that an authentically Catholic education is worth investing in. I think we're growing our tuition rate properly, but we can never lose sight of the financial concerns of our families. It's a scary thing for a family who loves Lourdes and wonders whether they will be able to continue to afford tuition as they have more children. I really

2. "Educator Interview: Heidi Altman," Catholic School Playbook website, https://www.catholicschoolplaybook.com/interview-heidi-altman.
3. "Educator Interview: Cyril Cruz," Catholic School Playbook website, https://www.catholicschoolplaybook.com/interview-cyril-cruz.

want to honor the domestic church and honor single-income families.[4]

FAMILY MODEL

Mo Woltering approaches tuition from the perspective that families—not students—pay tuition to be a part of his school community. Making it possible for all children in a family to attend the same K–12 school is the most significant motivation for his tuition model. He offers steep sibling discounts, such that a family with six or more children—including high school and lower school students—would pay less than $19,000. Because the rate for multiple children in a family is so low, Holy Family Academy only grants tuition assistance to approximately 8% of families.[5]

Offering a tuition schedule in harmony with Catholic teaching on openness to life is important to the leaders of faithful schools. Janice Martinez explains, "I think the sibling discount is important. We want to encourage fruitfulness in life. We want to support families that are open to life."

She credits her pastor and her parish for making Catholic education affordable for local families

4. "Educator Interview: Rosemary Vander Weele," Catholic School Playbook website, https://www.catholicschoolplaybook.com/interview-rosemary-vander-weele.

5. "Educator Interview: Mo Woltering," Catholic School Playbook website, https://www.catholicschoolplaybook.com/interview-mo-woltering.

attending her school. "Our pastor feels strongly that we should not turn anyone away," she says.[6]

Offering free tuition for the fourth child and additional children is a common practice of schools embracing the family model. Holy Child Catholic School (a parochial school in Tijeras, New Mexico), St. Augustine Academy (an independent school in Ventura, California), St. Regis Academy (a parochial school in Kansas City, Missouri), and St. Jerome Academy (a parochial school in Hyattsville, Maryland) are all K–8 schools that cap tuition after the third child.

Paul and Maura Doman are the parents of six children, with one on the way. They are passionate about education and consider the school they partner with to educate their children to be "definitely one of the most important decisions" they have had to make. For many years, they lived in northern Virginia, an area of the country known for excellent schools including several faithful Catholic schools. They were part of a strong Catholic school community in northern Virginia for several years.

Nonetheless, in 2018, the Domans moved thirty-five miles east to Hyattsville, Maryland, to enroll their children at St. Jerome Academy. The school's tuition model, which would enable them to educate all of their children at a fraction of the cost of other schools in the area, was a major factor in their decision. Three years later,

6. "Educator Interview: Janice Martinez," Catholic School Playbook website, https://www.catholicschoolplaybook.com/interview-janice-martinez.

they are "really happy" with their decision. "We have seen our kids grow in their faith and virtue and excel in their studies while attending St. Jerome Academy," they explain.[7]

The Domans are part of a growing movement of families who are willing to go to great lengths—by literally uprooting their lives and moving—to join one of the authentically Catholic school communities that are growing in number in the United States, but still not available in most locations. Affordability for large families is an important way these schools differentiate themselves and attract faithful families.

COMPETITIVE MODEL

When Jeffrey Presberg became headmaster of St. John the Beloved Academy, he set out to build a great school—a school that students, parents, and teachers would love, and that families would choose over "the best" schools in the area. His decades of experience as an educator and head of school at two independent schools informed his vision and strategic plan—including his approach to tuition. He had been the founding head-master of Western Academy in Houston, Texas, for five years, and the head of the lower school at The Heights School in Potomac, Maryland, for fifteen years. Western and The Heights are private liberal arts schools for boys

---

7. "Parent Interview: Paul & Maura Doman," Catholic School Play-book website, https://www.catholicschoolplaybook.com/interview-paul-maura-doman.

known for instilling in students a sense of adventure, intellectual curiosity, and moral virtue. Parents pay top dollar to send their sons to these schools to learn from, and be mentored by, an all-male faculty of strong, engaging teachers with high integrity. Tuition at Western Academy is $20,400 (grades 3–5) and $22,200 (grades 6–8). Tuition at The Heights is $23,284 (grades 3–5), $28,310 (grades 6–8), and $31,320 (grades 9–12). Neither Western nor The Heights offers sibling discounts. Both provide financial aid; nearly half of the students at The Heights receive financial aid. Both have full enrollment with waitlists.

He knew that charging five-figure tuition at a K–8 parochial school overseen by the diocese would be out of the question. But he also knew he needed to generate more revenue to invest in the school's teaching faculty and reverse plummeting enrollment. Teacher salaries are an expense Catholic schools did not have to worry about years ago when they were run by religious staff. He explains,

> Catholic schools are no longer staffed by religious workers. We now have laymen educating our children. We have to pay them. We can't have the mentality that teaching is a vocation of poverty. It's detrimental to what we're trying to accomplish. We have a beautiful, ambitious mission. We have the opportunity to save and transform the culture.

But we will fail if we cannot pay excellent teachers capable of inspiring their students.[8]

Part of his solution was to maintain modest tuition—$8,257 per student, with percentage increases each year (4–7%)—add book and activity fees, and phase out the sibling discount, which is currently approximately $1,000, with no increase per sibling and no children attending for free. This makes St. John the Beloved's per-student tuition on par with most parochial schools in the area, and considerably lower than most private schools. It also leaves families with one or two school-aged children mostly unaffected, although it may mean the students' peer group includes fewer children from large families. It probably also means some large families will choose a Catholic school with a more generous sibling discount over St. John the Beloved.

Changing the tuition model has significantly increased tuition revenue both because (1) enrollment is full, due to many changes at the school, and especially an increased investment in faculty hiring and training and (2) no children attend for free or for less than $7,000 (although some families do receive financial aid). Before Presberg became headmaster, tuition and fee revenue covered only 65% of the budget and families were fleeing; now it covers 80% of the budget and enrollment is full with a waitlist. Presberg is pursuing initiatives

8. "Educator Interview: Jeffrey Presberg," Catholic School Playbook website, https://www.catholicschoolplaybook.com/interview -jeffrey-presberg.

that will further strengthen the school through better fundraising.

Another leader who was determined to build a great school, and then set tuition according to revenue needs, is Peter Crawford of St. Jerome Institute. Similar to Presberg, he prioritized the development of his faculty as a primary consideration for his school. The result is a faculty he describes as "deeply committed, passionate, and talented," who "take the craft of teaching seriously," and who "have contributed to a unified vision" for the school.[9]

Tuition at SJI is $15,000, which is higher than many Catholic schools, but still considerably lower than most private schools in the area. SJI offers a modest sibling discount of $1,000 per student. Two years into the operation of the school, 95% of students received some form of tuition reduction, with an average grant of $5,000. Fundraising currently makes up the difference between tuition revenue and expenses, but as enrollment grows and SJI continues to solidify its reputation as a school that unleashes in students a love of learning within the Catholic tradition, Crawford expects tuition revenue to cover a greater share of operational expenses. Financial aid will continue to assist families, but the higher cost of tuition will enable SJI to receive the full amount from some families, and that should help maintain a stable school.

9. "Educator Interview: Peter Crawford," Catholic School Playbook website, https://www.catholicschoolplaybook.com/interview -peter-crawford.

EDUCATION CHOICE

Education choice could be a game-changer for Catholic schools struggling to increase enrollment and tuition revenue. Historically, parents who chose Catholic education for their children have had to pay twice: once for local district school through taxes and again to cover Catholic school tuition. But this is changing as more states embrace the idea that funding should follow students, not institutions.

Consider an illustration of how school choice in one state—West Virginia—makes Catholic education significantly more affordable for parents:

State without school choice	West Virginia's Education Savings Accounts (ESA)
Funding follows institutions	Funding follows students
Parents and other taxpayers pay into the system through property taxes and income taxes	Parents and other taxpayers pay into the system through property taxes and income taxes
A collective government fund is created for the purpose of distributing to public schools	A $4,600 ESA is created for each school-aged child*

Government distributed money to public schools	Parents decide how to spend each child's $4,600 ESA; options include public school costs, private school tuition, homeschooling costs, and other educational expenses
Parents can send children to public school for "free"	Parents can send children to public school for "free"
Parents can send children to private school, but they are responsible for 100% of the tuition	Parents can send children to private school and use up to $4,600 of each ESA toward tuition
Parents can homeschool, but they are responsible for 100% of costs	Parents can homeschool and use up to $4,600 of each ESA toward books, tutors, and other expenses

*ESAs are currently available to 90% of students in the state.[10]

Education choice could be transformative for Catholic schools because cost is a significant barrier for many families considering Catholic education. A study by the NCEA (National Catholic Education Association) and FADICA (Foundations and Donors Interested in Catholic Activities) found that "most American parents do not believe Catholic schools are affordable, and they

10. "Everything You Always Wanted to Know About School Choice (But Were Afraid to Ask)," Catholic School Playbook website, March 1, 2022, https://www.catholicschoolplaybook.com/post/everything-you-always -wanted-to-know-about-school-choice-but-were-afraid-to-ask.

are not confident they could afford the cost of tuition." The study further found that "awareness of state-sponsored tuition assistance programs" (e.g., school choice vouchers and tax credits) "is low, even among [families] living in states where they are offered."[11]

All Catholic school leaders—and all pastors of Catholic churches—should inform Catholic families about school choice programs in their state. As of March 2024, there are seventy-four programs in thirty-three states plus the District of Columbia and Puerto Rico that provide some level of private education choice. These include:

- **Fifteen with ESA programs**: Alabama, Arizona, Arkansas, Florida, Indiana, Iowa, Mississippi, Montana, Nevada, New Hampshire, North Carolina, South Carolina, Tennessee, Utah, and West Virginia
- **Fourteen with Voucher programs**: Arkansas, Georgia, Indiana, Louisiana, Maine, Maryland, Mississippi, New Hampshire, North Carolina, Ohio, Oklahoma, Utah, Vermont, and Wisconsin, plus District of Columbia and Puerto Rico
- **Two with Tax Credit ESAs**: Florida and Missouri
- **Nine with Individual Tuition Tax credits or deductions**: Alabama, Illinois, Indiana, Iowa,

11. "The Catholic School Choice: Understanding the Perspectives of Parents and Opportunities for More Engagement," FADICA and NCEA, December 2018, https://xbss.org/wp-content/uploads/2019/03/The-Catholic-School-Choice_National-Market-Research-Dec-2018.pdf.

Minnesota, Ohio, Oklahoma, South Carolina, and Wisconsin
- **Twenty-one with Scholarship Tax Credit programs**: Alabama, Arizona, Arkansas, Florida, Georgia, Indiana, Iowa, Kansas, Louisiana, Montana, Nebraska, Nevada, New Hampshire, Ohio, Oklahoma, Pennsylvania, Rhode Island, South Carolina, South Dakota, Utah, and Virginia

The following states offer no school choice as of March 2024:

- Alaska
- California
- Colorado
- Connecticut
- Delaware
- Hawaii
- Idaho
- Massachusetts
- Michigan
- New Jersey
- New Mexico
- New York
- North Dakota
- Oregon
- Texas
- Washington
- Wyoming

Momentum in the school choice movement is growing. 2021 was a breakthrough year. Eighteen states enacted seven new school choice programs—including West Virginia's groundbreaking ESA program—and expanded twenty-one existing programs. In 2023 and 2024, several states built on this momentum and expanded existing programs, added new ones, or went universal, meaning they expanded eligibility to every child regardless of income. At the time of this writing, ten states offer universal school choice and several more are on the verge of passing universal choice legislation. To borrow language from the business world, if the greatest challenge of most Catholic schools has been a mediocre, undifferentiated product, then finding customers who can afford the financing is a close second. School choice legislation is a crucial part of the solution to financing. Bishops, pastors, and school leaders can play a key role in helping their families to understand and prioritize this issue in their local elections, and alert their families to take advantage of the legislation once it is passed.

A reformer doing important work for school choice is Shawn Peterson, president of Catholic Education Partners, which works to ensure that any school choice legislation is friendly to Catholic schools and comes without strings attached. He sees the school choice movement and the future of the American Catholic Church as inextricably linked—which is why he encourages all Catholics to support school choice. He explains,

In his 1931 essay "The Schools," the great Catholic historian Hilaire Belloc said, "For upon the schools depends the continuance of the Faith." This statement is no less true today than it was nearly one hundred years ago when he wrote it. While many Catholic schools exist to provide that faithful education, existence does not equal access. We must work to ensure that all families who desire a truly Catholic education have the means to do so and the best way to ensure this is with robust education choice programs in every state. After all, the very future of the American Catholic Church is at stake.

FUNDRAISING

Most Catholic school principals and headmasters are educators at heart and administrators by necessity. Few have experience leading or managing projects outside of a school setting. Many learn to rely on their school networks to help them tackle unfamiliar challenges. This can lead to and exacerbate problems in many key areas, including one that is vital to the continued operation of a school: fundraising.

To keep the doors open, school leaders must bridge the gap between tuition revenue and costs. The amount school leaders must raise varies significantly from school to school, depending on a confluence of factors, including:

- Rate of enrollment
- Price of tuition
- Amount of discounts and financial aid granted
- Level of support (if any) from a parish or diocese
- Expenses of teacher and administrator salaries, lease or mortgage payments, academic resources, and capital projects

Although some Catholic schools—especially parochial schools that receive significant support from a parish—rely on fundraising to cover as much as 50% to 80% of the budget, most operate under a 70/30 to 85/15 tuition-to-fundraising model, where tuition covers 70% to 85% of the budget and fundraising covers the remaining 15% to 30%.

New schools often rely heavily on fundraising for the first few years of operation, when, by design, they may operate at only 20–25% enrollment. Indeed, it is not unusual for a start-up school to rely on fundraising for 50% to 60% of its revenue until it reaches full enrollment and can transition to a more traditional 70/30 to 85/15 tuition-to-fundraising model.

No two school leaders approach fundraising exactly the same way. But the most effective leaders incorporate the following elements into their fundraising strategy:

1. Dedicated staff
2. A thoughtful plan
3. Transparency and reporting
4. Major gifts

5. Campaigns
6. Events

In addition, Elisabeth Sullivan notes that schools involved in the reclaiming of the intellectual tradition of the Catholic Church have an advantage in fundraising over schools that hang onto secular models. She explains,

> Donors, too, are becoming increasingly attracted to Catholic schools in the classical liberal arts renewal, because they see that it works—not simply because it stabilizes the school but because it fosters a distinctly vibrant culture of faith and learning. *As so many young Catholics are falling away from the faith, they see that these schools are reversing the trend.* They are engines of evangelization, well worthy of investment.
>
> I am reminded of Pope Benedict XVI's statement during his US visit in 2008, about the unique system of Catholic education: "It provides a *highly commendable opportunity for the entire Catholic community to contribute generously to the financial needs of our institutions.* Their long-term sustainability must be assured. Indeed, everything possible must be done, in cooperation with the wider community, to ensure that they are accessible to people of all social and economic strata. No child should be denied his

or her right to an education in faith, which in turn nurtures the soul of a nation."[12]

DEDICATED STAFF

All effective school leaders understand that fundraising is an important part of their job—and one that cannot be fully delegated to other staff. That's because, as Crawford recognizes, a school leader is the "primary voice and face of fundraising" for a school and, as Vander Weele observes, "anyone considering supporting the school always wants to meet with [the school leader]."[13]

Donoghue recommends that school leaders embrace this crucial responsibility and also invest in a development director to assist with this important work. She explains, "If at all possible, schools and parishes should work with a development director who would be responsible for much of the groundwork of raising money. But leaders maintain an important position; they are often tasked with 'selling' the school's mission and vision to potential donors."[14]

Deacon Christopher Roberts has been the president and lead fundraiser of his school since the beginning. He says fundraising is an "endless job," but "rewarding." He

12. "Educator Interview: Elisabeth Sullivan," Catholic School Playbook website, https://www.catholicschoolplaybook.com/interview-elisabeth-sullivan.

13. "Peter Crawford"; "Rosemary Vander Weele."

14. "Mary Pat Donoghue."

explains, "On the best days, I'm telling the story of our school, building relationships, inviting people to participate in the mission, all while engaging with students and faculty and strengthening the internal life of the school. But that's a lot to do well every day."[15]

His school is transitioning from a start-up to a more established school. He now benefits from the help of a development director. Even so, he recognizes that there will "always" be a need for him to be involved in ongoing relationships with donors.

A THOUGHTFUL PLAN

Having a thoughtful plan—knowing what amount needs to be raised, through which efforts—is critical to the success of a school's fundraising efforts.

Generally, simple plans are easier for the school community to understand and get behind. An approach that has worked well for Woltering is budgeting for tuition and fees to cover general operating expenses, with fundraising revenue paying for improvements and capital campaigns.

Van Hecke's school utilizes a plan "of thirds" that has worked well for his school for decades. This means:

1. The office raises a third (personal relationships, foundations, direct mail).

15. "Educator Interview: Deacon Christopher Roberts," Catholic School Playbook website, https://www.catholicschoolplaybook.com/interview -christopher-roberts.

2. The board raises a third (gives or gets).
3. The parents raise a third through three events: a jog-a-thon (for families), a gala (run mostly by moms), and a golf-a-thon (run mostly by dads).

He says it's important to set attainable goals and use positive motivation to help all three groups feel challenged to meet their goals. Micromanaging, demanding the meeting of quotas, and "bean counting" are negative motivators that suppress morale and hinder performance. Also, he says it's counterproductive to overwork and overstimulate parents and community members with small fundraisers—for example, wrapping paper sales—that bring in small amounts. It's better to meet the small needs from the budget and allow the community to focus their energy on a few major events and initiatives.[16]

Fr. Robert Sirico agrees that fundraising efforts should be focused. He explains,

> We try to keep our fundraisers to a minimum. Constantly asking parents for more money throughout the year exhausts their patience and goodwill. Instead of a constant stream of small-scale fundraisers and intrusive capital campaigns, over the last few years we have striven to revive the Catholic duty to tithe. It is unfortunate to note that if Catholics

16. "Educator Interview: Michael Van Hecke," Catholic School Playbook website, https://www.catholicschoolplaybook.com/interview-michael-van-hecke.

tithed to the levels expected by Canon Law, the financial difficulties of the Church across the nation would disappear. By creating a community that our parishioners truly want to invest in, we hope to inspire a newfound desire to tithe in money, time, and prayer. This appeal is ongoing and is the primary way we seek to gain long-term financial security.[17]

Sacred Heart Academy's approach succeeds in raising 51% of its budget through fundraising, which keeps tuition affordable for families ($5,000 for K–8, $10,000 for 9–12).

TRANSPARENCY AND REPORTING

The better that parents and community members understand a school's fundraising needs, the more enthusiastic they will be about making gifts and volunteering their time to help a school reach its goals.

Donoghue advises school leaders to present an annual "State of the School" address to the community, outlining the school's financial state and upcoming initiatives.[18]

This approach was critical in helping Altman gain momentum for her school's fundraising early on. She credits providing "complete TRANSPARENCY in the

17. "Educator Interview: Fr. Robert Sirico," Catholic School Playbook website, https://www.catholicschoolplaybook.com/interview-fr-robert-sirico.

18. "Mary Pat Donoghue."

budget" with helping her build a "true partnership" with her community. She explains,

> First, I report the state of the school each year to our families. I engage them in the realities of offering this amazing educational program at an affordable price, and impress upon them the crucial role they play in making our "equation" work. I also explain this "equation" to our new families—so they understand from the beginning that this is a true partnership and a community effort. This seems to be the most effective way of inspiring the self-giving and the work it takes to maintain our fundraising efforts over the course of the year—and it also inspires them to help us find donors who will support our mission.
>
> I also show them all that we have done and continue to do to deliver a high-quality education, so that our families always know where their money is being spent. Whether it is new paint on the walls or new literature for their classrooms, our families know how money is spent. Transparency is key for families (and donors); they must have confidence that we are being good stewards of their treasure.[19]

19. "Heidi Altman."

MAJOR GIFTS

Donoghue observes that a weakness of traditional fundraisers is that they often "hit" the same people who are already paying tuition, without regard for giving capacity. Schools that have a major gifts program avoid this common problem by:

- Focusing on current families paying full tuition. As one parent shared, "Most parents paying full tuition are already doing some charitable giving. Many would gladly direct some of that charitable giving to the school that is serving their own children."
- Involving grandparents of current students, alumni families, and the wider community—of the parish, diocese, and friends of the school—in fundraising initiatives.

Van Hecke has developed a robust major gifts program over the course of decades. The essence of his program is "building friendships with many donors, large and small." He uses letters, visits to campus, and events to share the story of his school "with love and conviction." He emphasizes, "In order for this to work, though, the headmaster has to Tell the Story. He needs to also regularly encourage parents, students, and teachers to do the same. . . . The classical, the strong faith, and especially the palpable joy are all very attractive. We also clearly demonstrate how inexpensive our school is versus public schools or even high-priced private and Catholic schools. A simple chart can be a good story-telling aid."

Sending regular communications throughout the year—including some letters that ask for support and others that do not—help establish regular patterns of giving. Van Hecke says this enabled his fundraising program to build momentum early on. He shares a key piece of advice: "Do not underestimate the power of loving the small donor. She may send $10, but will also remember you in prayer. One early donor of ours was asked for $25 or $50—I cannot recall the original figure, but it was so small he could not say no. Five years later he donated $900,000."[20]

Vander Weele has had tremendous success engaging the broader community through her major gifts program. She says her school's mission—serving families by providing affordable Catholic education—resonates with all supporters of her school. Most of her donors have personal relationships with students or teachers. Some are invested in parish life. Some have grandchildren whom they hope will attend her school someday. A few years after she became principal, she started working with local Denver foundations and that is when "the scales tipped" for fundraising. "That happened," she says, "because people saw a Catholic school that was succeeding." She explains, *People are tired of supporting failing schools that produce ex-Catholics.* I accept

20. "Michael Van Hecke."

invitations to speak whenever I'm asked so more people can learn about our success and know not everything is doom and gloom."[21]

There was a time when most support for Catholic schools came from current and alumni families, but that is changing with the success of the Catholic liberal education movement. Now, many Catholics are eager to support schools capable of forming faithful, virtuous young people who understand and embrace the teachings of the Church. Roberts explains, "One interesting group of donors are older parents of grown children. They will never have kids at our school. They tell us they wish a school like ours had existed when their kids were younger. *They want to be a part of the renewal of the Church, and they see their support of our school as the way to do that.* There are a handful of younger donors who want our school to be here and thriving in a few years when their toddlers and elementary school students need us."[22]

CAMPAIGNS

A best practice of schools with strong fundraising programs is incorporating campaigns—fundraising initiatives that last for a period of time, often to raise money for a specific purpose—as a regular part of the life of the school.

21. "Rosemary Vander Weele."
22. "Deacon Christopher Roberts."

Crawford raises essential funds for his school by overseeing short campaigns during the school year, including:

- **Giving Week**: Over the course of a dedicated "Giving Week," he sends daily emails highlighting his school's unique and compelling culture and academic program. He sets a fundraising goal, reports on the school's progress throughout the week, and sends a celebratory email at the end of the week, thanking the community for its generosity. A matching gift—a pledge made by a supporter at the beginning of a campaign, promising to match all gifts up to a certain amount—has been an important part of his school's Giving Week.

- **Twelve Days of Christmas**: Throughout the twelve days of Christmas, he sends daily emails asking the community to support the purchase of specific items for the school—for example, lab equipment, a volleyball net, and materials to build a sailboat.

In association with these campaigns, and throughout the year, he also encourages community members to join the Society for the Renewal of the Catholic Mind, a membership society that acts as an intellectual community sponsored by the school. Gifts of $150 or more enroll a supporter in the Society.

Woltering relies on two campaigns every year to raise money and invite new people to participate in the life of the school:

- **Letter-Writing Campaign**: Families are asked to submit one to three names of family members and friends to receive a handwritten letter from the student, a picture of the student on campus, and a letter from Woltering providing an update on the school.
- **Directory Ad Campaign**: Families are given the option of making a $150 gift to the school or soliciting advertisements of at least $150 from local businesses for the annual family directory.

Martinez has found that the best way to secure necessary funds for her school is to pray about it and then appeal to parents and community members for help. This approach has worked as well for her capital campaign for a new building (she raised $450,000 in a few months) as it has for mini campaigns for a climbing rope for the playground (she raised $2,500 from parents by putting a note about it in the bulletin), a refrigerator for the school, and a sofa for the teachers' lounge.[23]

23. "Janice Martinez."

EVENTS

Fundraising events often serve the dual purpose of building community and raising essential funds for a school. Popular events include 5K races and "fun runs," golf tournaments, feast day celebrations, and galas.

When Altman became principal of her school, she transformed the major fundraising event of the year—the Spring Gala—by opening it up to the entire community and expanding it to include dinner and dancing with local bands. *She doubled the revenue of the gala the first year and increased it by 40% the next year.*

Presberg has similarly opened his events to the broader community, with great success. He explains, "We are building a culture where fundraising happens not only with current families but with the broader community. Our mission is bigger. *Our product is more than academics; it is the community of school and parish families. People are willing to support that.*"[24]

His most successful fundraising event is a Spring Dream Garden Party, "a relaxed cocktail party filled with conversation, friends, and music." In preparation for this event, he transforms the appearance of the school property to encourage guests to experience conversation and friendship—hallmarks of education at St. John the Beloved. He shares why attending to the details of the Spring Dream Garden Party is important: "How we do events matters. We think about the whole picture, from

24. "Jeffrey Presberg."

improving the look and feel of the school, to creating spaces for conversation. We are having success inviting community members to participate in the life of the school, so they feel a part of the mission."[25]

25. "Jeffrey Presberg."

CHAPTER 7

Overseers

THE HIGHEST LEVEL OF SUPPORT FOR A SCHOOL COMMUNITY

THE OVERSEERS OF A SCHOOL—a parish, diocese, or board of directors—can provide tremendous assistance to a school community by facilitating unique collaborative opportunities to strengthen all aspects of the operation of a school. It is not uncommon for leaders of thriving Catholic schools to credit supportive pastors, bishops, superintendents, and board members for providing essential help in key areas—especially recruiting and fundraising.

But the opposite is also true. Unsupportive overseers can weaken and even sabotage the success of a school. That's why school leaders and overseers must always strive to build and strengthen relationships with each other—and never lose sight of their mission of serving families and the Church. The best relationships are those where roles and responsibilities are understood—and subsidiarity is respected.

SUBSIDIARITY

Subsidiarity is a principle of Catholic social teaching requiring that decisions be made at the lowest level of an organization as possible, so that decision-makers are as close to the individuals who are affected by their actions as possible. Regarding the education of children in Catholic schools, the lowest-level decision-maker is the parent, followed by the teacher, followed by the school leader, followed by the overseers of the school. It is critical that all members of a school community understand how subsidiarity informs their relationships with each other. This means that:

- Parents provide for their children's spiritual, physical, emotional, and intellectual growth at home. They must model healthy habits, enforce discipline, and prepare children to respect the authority of their teachers. They should give teachers the opportunity to understand concerns and resolve conflicts before going "over the head" of the faculty to air grievances with the school leader.
- Teachers set the day-to-day priorities and activities of the classroom. They must communicate with parents about what they observe during the school day and how children can be better

supported at home. They should keep the school leader apprised of potentially problematic situations relating to students, families, and other teachers as they develop, and they should share concerns about the overall operation of the school with the school leader, only involving overseers as a last resort.

- School leaders advance the mission of the school by making all major operational decisions, including hiring teachers, recruiting families, managing the curriculum, and resolving conflicts. They should address problems with members of the school community in a timely manner. It is critical that they apprise the overseers of incidents and trends that undermine the mission of the school.

- Overseers provide the highest level of review and decision-making for a school. They examine benchmarks (enrollment data, financial statements, student test results, etc.), approve major projects, and supervise the work of the school leader. They should provide clear expectations and feedback to the school leader without micromanaging his or her work or otherwise interfering with the day-to-day operations of the school.

The principle of subsidiarity—and its application within a school community—should be established in writing and reinforced on a regular basis. School leaders should include guidelines for teachers and parents in an easily accessible handbook; pastors, bishops, and board members should include them in bylaws. School leaders should use back-to-school nights, newsletters, and other opportunities to emphasize the importance of subsidiarity. Overseers should take the time to have candid discussions with school leaders about what they should expect from the relationship, and they must be honest about past challenges and open to making changes that are in the best interests of the school.

GOVERNING WITH INTEGRITY

The overseers of a Catholic school must never lose sight of their purpose: to govern and strengthen the school, consistent with the teachings of the Catholic Church, in the service of school families and the universal Church. It is critical that overseers govern with integrity. They must take the time to understand the state of the school *as it actually is*, and take steps that they *reasonably believe will strengthen the school*.

Overseers should begin by collecting data from the last five to ten years. They should review:

- Total enrollment of families and students
- Number of families and students that applied for admission
- Number of families and students that left the school prematurely
- Average net tuition (amount actually paid) per student

- Survey results (especially Net Promoter Scores— see below)

ANNUAL SURVEY

School leaders should be in constant dialogue with parents and students throughout the school year to hear their perspective on what is going well and what needs to improve. This should be done in person when possible, but every channel—including phone and email—should be offered to parents because people differ in how they prefer to communicate.

In addition, schools should conduct an annual anonymous survey of parents that asks the same three questions every year:

1. On a scale of 0–10, how likely are you to recommend the school to a friend or family member?
2. What do you like the most about the school?
3. How can the school improve?

The first question is taken from the business world and solicits what is commonly referred to as the Net Promoter Score. It is one of the most common survey questions employed by businesses to monitor customer satisfaction over time. The advantage of using an eleven-point scale as opposed to a simple Yes/No answer is that it is more likely to capture whether respondents are enthusiastic enough to promote the school within their personal network. Answers of 9 or 10 are the goal;

they represent parents who are most likely to refer future families. Answers of 7 or 8 are considered neutral and are generally discarded. Answers of 6 and below signal that parents are at risk of leaving the school and even dissuading others from staying or joining. Schools should monitor the ratio of 9s and 10s to 6s and below, and work to improve that ratio year over year.

There are five main benefits to collecting data using this survey:

- It gives schools a standard metric to track progress over time to better understand how well parents think their children are being served.
- It motivates school leaders, staff, and teachers to constantly improve.
- It alerts school leaders to problems that need to be addressed—this includes sensitive and serious problems that may not be revealed without the anonymity of a survey—and gives them something concrete to present to staff and teachers to initiate difficult discussions.
- It alerts school leaders to perceived problems and provides opportunities to explain and clarify strengths of the school that may be misunderstood by some members of the school community.
- Schools that perform well can use the data in their messaging and marketing materials for recruiting and fundraising.

Surveys should be conducted in the spring or summer so answers can be based on experiences covering most of the school year. Online surveys offer user-friendly formats that may increase participation and allow for easier, more accurate data collection as compared to paper surveys.

It takes a courageous school leader to administer a Net Promoter Score survey every year. Most schools fear the results and shy away from such feedback and metrics. It is worth noting that not all complaints and suggestions are worthy of being addressed; those that would compromise the mission and culture of the school suggest a breakdown in the admissions process and highlight the importance of recruiting families and students who support the school's goals.[1]

FULFILLING OVERSEER RESPONSIBILITIES

If the data signal weaknesses or problems, the school's overseers must confront them head on. Specifically, they must ask: "What is our school *not doing*, that stronger schools—especially those with full enrollment—*are doing*?" One way to find out is by reading this playbook, taking notes on ideas and approaches not being implemented, and then discussing the future of the school with the school leader. Overseers need to be willing to

---

1. Michael Ortner, "How Catholic Schools Can Steal a Key Metric from the Business World," Catholic School Playbook website, February 15, 2022, https://www.catholicschoolplaybook.com/post/how-catholic-schools-can-steal-a-key-metric-from-the-business-world.

replace school leaders who lack the will, skill, or fortitude to do what is needed to rebuild a school.

Overseers who are serious about reversing declining enrollment need to set clear and realistic expectations of a school leader. This requires: (1) admitting problems, (2) supporting a school leader's reasonable plan to address problems head on, and (3) holding the school leader accountable. A school leader who enjoys the support of overseers to make major changes to strengthen a school—including changes to the curriculum and faculty—should be required to show progress through regular updates. Overseers should be prepared to replace a school leader who fails to show considerable progress after two or three years.

At the same time, overseers must do their part. In addition to supporting the school leader, overseers should:

- Promote the school within their sphere of influence. For example, pastors should have conversations with parents about their children's education and allow school leaders to speak after Mass. Board members of independent schools should invite likeminded friends to open houses and other events.
- Help raise money for the school. For example, pastors should introduce school leaders to parishioners who give generously to the parish. Board members of independent schools should include the school in their charitable giving; they

should also help make connections for school leaders and invite likeminded friends to fundraising events.

PAROCHIAL SCHOOLS AND PASTORS

Pastors often serve as the most important partner to the leader of a parochial school. The most supportive pastors provide spiritual guidance to the school community, allocate parish resources to be used by the school, encourage parish families to enroll at the school, and serve in multiple capacities to assist a school leader in promoting and raising money for the school.

Reflecting on his experience with Sacred Heart Academy, Fr. Robert Sirico says a pastor does not need administrative experience to be an effective leader of a Catholic school. When he arrived at his parish, he had no experience working in Catholic education. But he had what he describes as the indispensable trait of a pastor: the ability to articulate a vision and inspire the right people to get involved. He warns that pastors can be tempted to try to do everything themselves, which is exhausting and fails to build a team of strong leaders. He encourages pastors to focus their energy on involving the school in greater pastoral efforts, preaching the Gospel, and getting people to heaven.

Not all pastors are as thoughtful, energetic, and entrepreneurial as Fr. Sirico. Some resent the additional responsibilities that come with having a school connected to their parishes. Some lack the disposition to work well with a school leader. Some limit their engagement with schools because of prior bad experiences with the staff of Catholic schools.

School leaders should understand that not all situations are ideal, but all can be improved with time and effort. Heidi Altman says that when a pastor lacks enthusiasm, it is the principal's job to continue to be the advocate for the school and find support from others in the school community and diocese. But even then, the principal should make a good faith effort to keep the pastor apprised of plans for the school. She explains, "Keep in mind that change is harder for some people than others, and we therefore must be ready to spend a lot of time just sitting down and talking to one another, constantly communicating the vision."

Altman shares that, even before she announced her school's renewal, she spent a lot of time with her pastor, as well as her superintendent, faculty, advisory board, and influential parents, discussing why the change was needed, how the school was going to be different than other schools, and what it was going to look like. This was time well spent. Altman explains, "Once we all started speaking that same language, it became easier to spread the vision to others—then we could all hop into the same boat and start rowing in the same direction!"[2]

2. "Educator Interview: Heidi Altman," Catholic School Playbook website, https://www.catholicschoolplaybook.com/interview-heidi-altman.

Once everyone is "rowing in the same direction," it's still important for a school leader to continue to cultivate a relationship with the pastor. Rosemary Vander Weele credits her weekly meetings, "even when there is nothing critical to discuss," with keeping her relationship with her pastor strong. She explains, "It's important for us to have that touch point. He's one priest of a huge parish so he can't be here all the time. He is present as much as possible, but, even more important than his presence, is his unspoken support. He and I are very much in lockstep."[3]

DIOCESAN SCHOOLS AND SUPERINTENDENTS OF CATHOLIC SCHOOLS

Diocesan schools benefit from the financial support and endorsement of the diocese. In exchange, they are generally required to adopt a set of standards and benchmarks that are not significantly different from those used by modern secular schools. For several years, many dioceses struggled to adapt to the breakthrough success of the renewal of Catholic liberal education. But that has changed. Thanks to school leaders who have put in the time and effort to work through questions and concerns by superintendents and other diocesan staff, there is now precedent for dioceses to grant greater autonomy to renewed Catholic schools.

3. "Educator Interview: Rosemary Vander Weele," Catholic School Playbook website, https://www.catholicschoolplaybook.com/interview -rosemary-vander-weele.

St. Jerome Academy was the first diocesan school to work out such an agreement with the superintendent of Catholic schools of a diocese. Since 2010, the school has followed its own Educational Plan. Rather than begrudge the school's departure from diocesan standards, the diocese now celebrates it as the reason for the school's turnaround success. Consider this description of the school on the Archdiocese of Washington website: "St. Jerome Academy is the Archdiocese's Classical school and one of only a few schools nationwide to pair a liberal-arts based K–8 curriculum with a Montessori pre-K program. Our school is dedicated to the cultivation of truth, goodness, and beauty in every child. The SJA Educational Plan was implemented in the 2010–2011 school year, after years of declining enrollment. Following several straight years of dramatic growth, SJA is now at full enrollment and attracts 175–200 applicants per year."[4]

Altman has a strong relationship with the Diocese of Austin. She was intentional about involving the superintendent of Catholic schools in her plans to transform her school. One of her goals has been to provide a roadmap for other schools in the diocese to embrace Catholic liberal education. She recalls,

> In my diocese . . . we wanted to be sure that we tackled some major challenges head-on so that it

---

4. "Saint Jerome Academy," Archdiocese of Washington website, https://adwcatholicschools.org/schools/saint-jerome-academy/.

would be easier if other schools wanted to join us on our journey; hence my amazing dean of curriculum worked on classical standards that could be used with our accreditation agency for schools like us. We now are going to meet regularly with that agency, along with our wonderfully supportive superintendent, to further develop other aspects of our accreditation process that would allow us to engage in continuous improvement with the freedom to operate in a classical model.[5]

Vander Weele has a relationship with the Archdiocese of Denver that is a true partnership. The superintendent has actively sought out Vander Weele and her school community for guidance on how to accommodate and support Catholic liberal education in Denver. She explains,

Our relationship with the diocese is also critical. The current superintendent is the third in that position since I've been at Lourdes. He is the first who fully supports what we're doing. The first two took a hands-off approach. But now, the office of Catholic schools is incredibly supportive. They appreciate what we're doing, have sought us out for advice and guidance, and have been accommodating about not imposing bureaucratic requirements that don't work for us. For example, they know we don't have devices

5. "Heidi Altman."

for every student, so we take standardized tests manually. It's been a big help having the freedom to satisfy the requirements of the diocese in a way that is consistent with our approach.[6]

INDEPENDENT SCHOOLS AND BOARDS OF DIRECTORS

Independent schools are governed by a board of directors that serves as the legal entity overseeing the school. Most board members are not involved in the day-to-day operation of the school, and yet they have enormous power over the most consequential matters concerning a school—for example, changes to the mission and vision, updates to major policies, the hiring and supervision of a school leader, and the purchase of property. It is critical, therefore, that the right people serve on the board—and that problems regarding the healthy functioning of the board are identified and addressed as early and as constructively as possible.

Selecting a board is one of the first tasks completed by the founders of a new school. Often the parents starting a school make up the initial board. It is not uncommon for the board to experience high turnover in the first few years until a core group of members who work well together is established. The process of developing the board—by inviting new members to join

6. "Rosemary Vander Weele."

and rotating weak or problematic members off—can be overwhelming. Observing three general guidelines is helpful:

- The board should only consist of individuals who are aligned philosophically with the mission of the school, passionate about advancing a clear vision for the school, and endowed with personal attributes necessary to govern with integrity.
- Individuals are unfit for the board unless they are known to be honest, gracious, reasonable, willing to listen and learn, and capable of putting the good of the school over personal agendas.
- It should never be assumed that successful adults who have an association with the school—for example, who have a child or grandchild enrolled at the school—share the values of the school leadership and have the appropriate disposition to contribute to the positive governance of the school. New members must be carefully vetted before they are invited to join the board.

In addition to finding the right individuals to serve, boards should consider policies and practices that have worked well for independent Catholic schools, including:

- The head of school should have a seat on the board. It is inappropriate for the board to meet and not communicate decisions made to the head of school. It is unhelpful for the head of school not to hear and participate in discussions shaping important decisions.

- Per the principle of subsidiarity (discussed earlier in the chapter), the board should allow the head of school to run the day-to-day operations of the school.
- The board should establish committees to facilitate greater assistance in important areas—for example, admissions, fundraising, hiring, curriculum development, and Catholic formation. Committees can include faculty members and other non-board members. Inviting someone to serve on a committee is a good way to audition outsiders for board membership.
- The full board should meet at least quarterly; committees can meet separately in between meetings of the full board.
- Not all board members must be major donors, but all must give at a level that is appropriate for their situation. As one school leader put it: "100% board giving is non-negotiable. Why should donors do what the board is unwilling to do?"[7]
- The board should strive to maintain institutional memory among board members. One way to do this is by not having fixed terms. Another way is to reappoint strong members upon the completion of a term.

7. "Educator Interview: Julian Malcolm," Catholic School Playbook website, https://www.catholicschoolplaybook.com/interview-julian -malcolm.

- In recognition of the importance of strong and principled leadership, the board should have a policy of facilitating the removal of ineffective or problematic board members.

School leaders have an important role to play in helping the board provide responsible governance. Their job is to communicate effectively with the board so decisions can be based not on a theoretical idea about the way a school could be run but on the lived reality of the school community they serve. This means school leaders should prepare regular reports and make themselves available to answer questions. It also means they should proactively encourage the board to participate in the life of the school. Peter Crawford, who has had a strong relationship with his board since the founding of his school, explains, "It is important that a school not see its board as an alien entity, that it encourages the board to witness the life of the school and foster a relationship of trust with board members."[8] He recommends encouraging board members to visit the school, sit in classrooms, and get a firsthand experience of the school. Ultimately, all interactions should be aimed at helping the board work together professionally, in a spirit of friendship, to serve the good of the school.

8. "Educator Interview: Peter Crawford," Catholic School Playbook website, https://www.catholicschoolplaybook.com/interview-peter-crawford.

Answering the Call

THE HUNDREDS OF CATHOLIC SCHOOLS across the country that have fully embraced their rich Catholic heritage are providing renewed hope for the Catholic Church. They are helping to form a new generation of Catholics who are wise and faithful followers of Jesus; they are causing entire families to discover the truth, goodness, and beauty of Church traditions; and they are leading a revival of religious vocations. This renewal of the mission, curriculum, pedagogy, and teacher communities within Catholic schools is accompanied by further good news. More Americans have realized the importance of the school choice movement, and great progress has been made in passing school choice legislation in a growing number of states. This means that parents who choose to send their children to Catholic schools can redirect their tax money that would have gone to the secular public neighborhood school to the Catholic school of their own choosing. They will no longer have to "double pay," and this will allow all families—regardless of income—to have the financial means to send their children to any school they choose.

The schools and school leaders featured in *The Catholic School Playbook* are by no means perfect. Some level of dysfunction accompanies every human institution, and each school profiled here will no doubt always remain, to varying degrees, a work in progress. What sets them apart from other Catholic schools is not merely their enrollment or financial success; rather, it is primarily their vision, their embrace of the Catholic intellectual tradition, and the witness of their faculty community. We are deeply grateful to the individuals who have shared their stories, knowing that it may invite scrutiny, and we are delighted by the success of the schools included herein and all the schools at the forefront of the renewal movement.

It would be a terrible mistake to believe that the renewal of authentically Catholic, classically liberal education is merely a niche market—just one school model among many that may be fine for a small minority of Catholic families and schools but not for others. Every child deserves a formative education in which their sense of wonder is nurtured; their virtues, particularly their intellectual virtues, are developed; and their longings to seek the truth, desire the good, and love the beautiful are cultivated.

It would also be a mistake to assume that the Catholic education renewal that is currently underway is a finished product with no room for continued innovation. Michael Hanby reminds us that "none of us have the benefit of having been formed by a genuinely Catholic culture, and few of us have the kind of education that we are hoping to give our children. The movement therefore has something of an 'experimental' quality. It's a long process of trial and error and the errors are okay, and in fact an improvement on what our culture has to offer."

This playbook is a clarion call for all bishops, superintendents, school leaders, and parents to raise our collective expectations for what we desire our Catholic schools to provide our children who deserve a Catholic education that is both spiritually and intellectually Catholic.

How do you even get started? Here are three steps to gain some early traction:

1. **Get everyone on board and excited for a bold, authentically Catholic vision of education for their children.** Share *The Catholic School Playbook* with parents, school leaders, and yes, even your bishop. The whole book is freely available online! Read and discuss it. Reach out to school leaders to ask them questions about their experiences and challenges. Visit schools like St. Jerome Institute in Washington, DC, and Our Lady of Lourdes Catholic Classical School in Denver, Colorado, or find schools that are part of the renewal near you to witness firsthand what this sort of education looks like in practice.

2. **Contact the nonprofits that are serving the renewal movement so you can benefit from their many years of experience.** The Institute for Catholic Liberal Education provides teacher training and hosts events for teachers, school leaders, superintendents, and bishops. Cana Academy offers workshops to high school teachers to help them lead more effective and engaging great books seminars. They also publish teacher guides for leading discussions on classic texts ranging from Plato's *Apology* and Aristotle's *Ethics* to Dante's *Inferno* and Dostoevsky's *Brothers Karamazov*. The Augustine Institute recently launched a Master of Arts program in Catholic Education that you can do in person or remotely, full-time or part-time.

3. **Create a strategic plan with clear, measurable goals.** It needs to include a plan for renewing the mission, culture, and curriculum of the school, a recruiting and training plan for teachers, and a marketing plan for attracting the right families. Perhaps most importantly, it needs a leader who both gets the vision and understands how to execute the plan, hire great people, and provide them the guidance that they need. This goes for the pastor or school board hiring the right leader for a school as well as for the bishop hiring the right superintendent to oversee many schools.

School does not have to be the wonder-killing, intellectually mediocre experience that it was for the vast majority of us. Catholic schools have an opportunity to lead the way, not only in forming the souls of the next generation, but also in bringing about a renewal in both the Church and society at large. May all people entrusted with the education and formation of God's children have the strength and grace to answer his call!

Required Classics

IF YOU WENT TO CATHOLIC HIGH SCHOOL and you weren't required to read Augustine's *Confessions*, Aquinas' *Treatise on Law*, or Dante's *Inferno*, then you should ask for a refund. You were robbed! Every school will have a different reading list, and that's to be expected. There is no shortage of amazing reading lists that mention hundreds or even thousands of books worth reading. But there are some texts that are so excellent, so insightful about the human experience, or so important to the history of ideas, that they rise to the level of a classic that must be read and discussed if you want to consider yourself well-educated. Some of these classic texts are written by faithful Catholics. Others are completely contrary to Catholic thought but should still be read to understand their influence. The following short list is our attempt at capturing the classic texts that absolutely should be included as required reading of every student attending Catholic school.

HIGH SCHOOL

Expository Literature
Bible (selections)
Thucydides, *History of the Peloponnesian War*
Plato, *Apology, Crito, Gorgias, Meno, Phaedo, Republic*
Aristotle, *Nicomachean Ethics*
Cicero, *De Officiis*
Athanasius, *On the Incarnation*
Augustine, *Confessions*
Thomas Aquinas, *Summa theologiae* (specifically the Five Proofs for the Existence of God and the *Treatise on Law*)
Dante, *Divine Comedy*
Michel de Montaigne, *An Apology for Raymond Sebond*
René Descartes, *Meditations on First Philosophy*
Thomas Hobbes, *Leviathan* (selections)
John Locke, *Second Treatise on Civil Government*
Jean-Jacques Rousseau, *Discourse on Inequality, On the Social Contract*
Edmund Burke, *Reflections on the Revolution in France*
Alexis de Tocqueville, *Democracy in America* (selections)
Georg Wilhelm Friedrich Hegel, *Reason in History*
Karl Marx, *The Communist Manifesto*
John Stuart Mill, *On Liberty*

Imaginative Literature

Homer, *Iliad*, *Odyssey*

Aeschylus, *Oresteia*

Sophocles, *Antigone*

Virgil, *Aeneid*

William Shakespeare, *Hamlet*, *King Lear*, *Macbeth*

Jane Austen, *Pride and Prejudice*

Charles Dickens, *A Tale of Two Cities*

Fyodor Dostoyevsky, *The Brothers Karamazov*,
  Crime and Punishment

George Orwell, *Animal Farm*

Robert Bolt, *A Man for All Seasons*

American Literature

Declaration of Independence

Constitution of the United States

The Federalist Papers (1, 2, 9, 10, 14, 15, 23, 31, 33,
  39, 41, 51, 78)

Frederick Douglass, *Narrative of the Life of Frederick
  Douglass*

Henry David Thoreau, "Civil Disobedience,"
  Walden

Mark Twain, *The Adventures of Huckleberry Finn*

Willa Cather, *My Antonia*

Ernest Hemingway, *The Old Man and the Sea*

Harper Lee, *To Kill a Mockingbird*

Martin Luther King Jr., *Letter from Birmingham Jail*

Flannery O'Connor, *The Complete Stories*
  (selections)

That's over fifty classics—some of which can be read in a short evening, while others require intensive reading over several weeks—to be read over the four years of high school. Ideally, we should all encounter these texts for the first time in high school, revisit many of them in college, and then return to them over the course of our lifetime. It's also important to note that many of them require the guidance of a good teacher to penetrate their deeper meaning, or even to simply enjoy them.

KINDERGARTEN–8TH GRADE

Ideally, before students get to the "great books," they should encounter good books—largely children's classics that are some of the greatest stories ever told. We limited each grade to just three to four classics, which gives plenty of opportunity for school leadership to select even more stories—often by the same authors—that capture the imaginations of their students.

Eighth Grade
Louisa May Alcott, *Little Women*, *Little Men*
St. Thérèse of Lisieux, *Story of a Soul*
J.R.R. Tolkien, *The Lord of the Rings*

Seventh Grade
Charles Dickens, *A Christmas Carol*
Jack Schaefer, *Shane*
Mark Twain, *The Adventures of Tom Sawyer*
Jules Verne, *The Mysterious Island*

Sixth Grade
Richard Adams, *Watership Down*
Lucy Maud Montgomery, *Anne of Green Gables*
E. Nesbit, *The Railway Children*
J.R.R. Tolkien, *The Hobbit*

Fifth Grade
Frances Hodgson Burnett, *A Little Princess*
Esther Forbes, *Johnny Tremain*
Jack London, *The Call of the Wild*
Wilson Rawls, *Where the Red Fern Grows*

Fourth Grade
C.S. Lewis, *The Chronicles of Narnia*
Robert McCloskey, *Homer Price*
Johanna Spyri, *Heidi*
Robert Louis Stevenson, *Treasure Island*

Third Grade
Rudyard Kipling, *The Jungle Book*
E.B. White, *Charlotte's Web*
Laura Ingalls Wilder, *Little House on the Prairie*

Second Grade
Aesop's Fables
Arnold Lobel, *Frog and Toad Are Friends*
George MacDonald, *The Princess and the Goblin*
Maryknoll Sisters, *Catholic Children's Treasure Box*

**Kindergarten and First Grade
(mostly read-aloud)**

The Golden Children's Bible

Hans Christian Andersen, *Classic Fairy Tales*

Ingri and Edgar Parin d'Aulaire, *D'Aulaires' Book of Greek Myths*

Paul Galdone, *The Little Red Hen*

A.A. Milne, *The Complete Tales of Winnie-the-Pooh*

Else Holmelund Minarik, *Little Bear*

Beatrix Potter, *The Tale of Peter Rabbit*

Dr. Seuss, *Green Eggs and Ham*

Note to parents: When choosing a school for your child, be sure to ask what their required reading list is for each grade. The books that make their list will tell you a lot about the leadership, vision, and principles of the school. If your school does not require one of the books listed at the K–8 level, then they also make great summer reading!

WORD ON FIRE

In a world full of noise and distraction, form your
imagination with beauty, truth, and goodness!

Word on Fire Votive is a new imprint for children that
publishes inspiring stories with stunning illustrations
designed to turn young hearts to the Gospel.

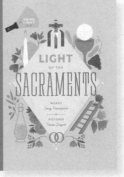

To learn more about our other Votive books, visit

wordonfire.org/votive

What is classical Catholic education?

Through brief vignettes, personal anecdotes from students and teachers, and examples from the classroom, *Know Thyself* makes a positive case for an education journey that teaches students to see themselves through God's eyes—and to truly know themselves and who they are called to be.

Get the book at

wordonfire.org/know